RICHARD F. HUBBARD & JEFFREY L. RODENGEN

Edited by Heather Deeley
Design and layout by Sandy Cruz and Rachelle Donley

In loving memory of Francis Hubbard;
May his kind spirit soar above us always

—Richard F. Hubbard

Write Stuff Enterprises, Inc.
1001 South Andrews Avenue,
Second Floor
Fort Lauderdale, FL 33316
1-800-900-Book (1-800-900-2665)
(954) 462-6657
www.writestuffbooks.com

Publisher's Cataloging in Publication

Hubbard, Richard F.
    Biomet—from Warsaw to the World / Richard
F. Hubbard & Jeffrey L. Rodengen.—1st ed.
    p. cm.
    Includes bibliographical references and index.
    LCCN 20001135035
    ISBN 0-945903-86-3

    1. Biomet Inc.—History. 2. Orthopedic apparatus
industry—United States. 3. Orthopedic implants
industry—United States I Rodengen, Jeffrey L.
II. Title.

HD9995.O74B56 2002   338.7'681761
                      QBI02-200475

Library of Congress
Catalog Card Number 20001135035

ISBN 0-945903-86-3

Completely produced in the
United States of America
10 9 8 7 6 5 4 3 2 1

Also by Jeffrey L. Rodengen

The Legend of Chris-Craft

IRON FIST: The Lives of Carl Kiekhaefer

Evinrude-Johnson and The Legend of OMC

Serving the Silent Service: The Legend of Electric Boat

The Legend of Dr Pepper/Seven-Up

The Legend of Honeywell

The Legend of Ingersoll-Rand

The Legend of Briggs & Stratton

The Legend of Stanley: 150 Years of The Stanley Works

The MicroAge Way

The Legend of Halliburton

The Legend of York International

The Legend of Nucor Corporation

The Legend of Goodyear: The First 100 Years

The Legend of AMP

The Legend of Cessna

The Legend of VF Corporation

The Spirit of AMD

The Legend of Rowan

New Horizons: The Story of Ashland Inc.

The History of American Standard

The Legend of Mercury Marine

The Legend of Federal-Mogul

Against the Odds: Inter-Tel—The First 30 Years

The Legend of Pfizer

State of the Heart: The Practical Guide to Your Heart and Heart Surgery
with Larry W. Stephenson, M.D.

The Legend of Worthington Industries

The Legend of Trinity Industries, Inc.

The Legend of IBP, Inc.

The Legend of Cornelius Vanderbilt Whitney

The Legend of Amdahl

The Legend of Litton Industries

The Legend of Bertram
with David A. Patten

The Legend of Gulfstream

The Legend of ALLTEL
with David A. Patten

The Yes, you can of Invacare Corporation
with Anthony L. Wall

The Legend of Ritchie Bros. Auctioneers

The Ship in the Balloon: The Story of Boston Scientific and the Development of Less-Invasive Medicine

The Legend of Day & Zimmermann

The Legend of Noble Drilling

Fifty Years of Innovation: Kulicke & Soffa

TABLE OF CONTENTS

INTRODUCTION

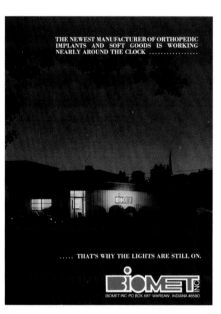

THE NEWEST MANUFACTURER OF ORTHOPEDIC IMPLANTS AND SOFT GOODS IS WORKING NEARLY AROUND THE CLOCK . . . .

. . . . . THAT'S WHY THE LIGHTS ARE STILL ON.

BIOMET INC
BIOMET INC. PO BOX 587· WARSAW, INDIANA 46580

BIOMET WAS FOUNDED by four men who had learned a valuable lesson in larger corporations: how *not* to do things.

"We saw how easy it was for the competition to be successful *without* being efficient," said cofounder Dane A. Miller, Ph.D.

Biomet is headquartered in Warsaw, Indiana, the orthopedic capital of the world. Forming the company was a risky venture for the cofounders and their wives, for they would face formidable competition from firmly established market leaders. The new company in town had very specific goals: be the most responsive orthopedic supplier of the highest quality, clinically proven products on the market, and never lose sight of the integrity and spirit of teamwork.

To reach its goals, Biomet took suggestions from surgeons and produced improved implants faster than its large competitors could. It also identified the needs of surgeons and patients and worked closely with sales representatives to meet those needs.

Nearly 25 years after its inception, Biomet has retained its goals. It is a company that has experienced great success and stayed true to its small-company values.

Biomet's unique personality surfaced early: The dress is casual, the doors to all offices are open, and memos are virtually nonexistent. In fact, Biomet's corporate culture is rather anticorporate. And its founders don't sit on the sidelines—especially when it comes to fun and games.

President and CEO Dane Miller has been known to sit in the dunking cage at company picnics. Chairman Niles Noblitt has competed in the potato sack race. Vice Chairman Jerry Ferguson has tooled around the parking lot in a race car emblazoned with the Biomet logo. And apparently board member Ray Harroff has had his share of difficulty distinguishing between mud puddles and gullies—after a heavy rain once, he drove a 1978 green Datsun station wagon (a company car) into water up to its windows.

The men and women who work at Biomet are team members, not employees, and they live out the fellowship and playful spirit of Biomet. They have held a wedding in one of the break rooms, competed in ugly tie contests, and come to work dressed for every occasion, from Halloween to Hawaiian Shirt Day. One team member comes to work dressed as Elvis when the mood strikes him.

While Biomet's philosophy and culture have remained intact, much has changed since the company's modest debut in 1978, when, working out of a converted barn, it registered sales of $17,000. It broke the $1 billion barrier in 2000.

Biomet and its subsidiaries design, manufacture, and market products used primarily by musculoskeletal medical specialists in both surgical and nonsurgical therapy. These include reconstructive and fixation devices, electrical bone growth stimulators, orthopedic support devices, operating room supplies, general surgical instruments, arthroscopy products, spinal products, bone cements, bone substitute materials, craniomaxillofacial implants and instruments, and dental reconstructive implants. Biomet has more than 750 issued and pending patents. It operates manufacturing and office facilities in more than 50 locations worldwide and distributes its products in more than 100 countries.

Biomet—From Warsaw to the World commemorates the integrity and innovative nature of the company's founders as well as the people who have joined the team.

Biomet embodies an aggressive devotion to its values, faith in technological innovation, and outstanding service, and these are the keys to its success. When hospitals began to challenge suppliers to lower their prices in the early 1990s, Biomet did not give in. When the industry was turned upside down by price pressures, consolidation, and national contracting, Biomet never lost sight of the importance of product innovation, the critical role of its sales representatives, and the right of a surgeon to choose the best product.

As the average life span increases, more people turn to musculoskeletal procedures to improve their quality of life—in 2001, one in four of us faced some type of musculoskeletal injury or disorder. Biomet innovations cut the length of hospital stay and reduce the number of operations. With a strong reputation as one of the fastest growing and best-managed companies in the world, the Biomet team looks forward to a healthy future.

ACKNOWLEDGMENTS

A GREAT NUMBER OF people assisted in the research, preparation, and publication of *Biomet—From Warsaw to the World.*

The authors would like to extend our gratitude to research assistants Anthony DeBartolo and Michael Williams.

Special thanks are due to Biomet cofounder Dane Miller, Ph.D., president and CEO, for the generous donation of his time and invaluable insight. Cofounders Niles Noblitt, chairman, Jerry Ferguson, vice chairman, and Ray Harroff, board member, also provided keen observations about Biomet's operating culture and history.

Barbara Goslee, corporate communications manager, and Terry Armstrong, manager of marketing communications, provided valuable help. Craig Koble, graphic designer, created the book's front cover.

Many Biomet team members and retirees greatly enriched the book by discussing their experiences at the company. The authors extend particular gratitude to these men and women for their candid recollections and anecdotes:

Barb Akers, regulatory specialist; Tom Allen, vice president of international operations in the Americas and Asia Pacific; Jim Babcock, marketing director for trauma products; Ron Bateman, retired Biomet-Merck development manager; Keith Beaty, cochairman of 3i; Ken Beres, M.D., vice president of regulatory affairs; Craig Blaschke, vice president of biomaterials technology; Don Boggs, retired director of manufacturing; Bob Border, senior development engineer in trauma; Rich Borror, vice president of manufacturing; David Brown, development engineer in patient-matched implants; Dan Cordill, hip manufacturing senior engineer; John Deming, retired project engineer; Ted Dobbins, general maintenance; Garry England, senior vice president of Warsaw operations; Norma Ferguson; Tony Fleming, vice president of research and development; Greg Garber, director of flight operations; Dean Golden, director of biomaterials manufacturing; Jim Haller, vice president of finance; Daniel Hann, senior vice president, general counsel, and secretary; Rose Harroff, retired director of soft goods; Greg Hartman, senior vice president of finance, treasurer, and CFO; Troy Hershberger, director of product development for hips and knees; Joel Higgins, director of resorbable engineering; Paula Hoesel, regulatory affairs coordinator; Bill Kolter, vice president of marketing; Susan Konkle, purchasing supervisor; Eric Martin, director of corporate sales; Terry Martin, director of manufacturing engineering; John McDaniel, retired engineer; Cheryl McIntosh, accounting manager; Jerry Miller, board member; Kenneth Miller, board member; Mary Louise Miller; Dave Montgomery, vice president of sales; Chuck Niemier, senior vice president of international operations; Nancy Noblitt; James Pastena, president of EBI and vice president of Biomet; Lance Perry, marketing director for knee reconstruction; Joel Pratt, president of Lorenz Surgical and senior vice president of Biomet; Lee Ritchey, tool crib production control manager; Robert Ronk, director of biomaterials engineering; Greg Sasso, vice president of corporate development and communications; Steve Stewart, director of sales administration; Delmas Stiles, trauma senior supervisor; Kevin Stone, director of product development; Sam Stutzman, director of manufacturing; John Susaraba, marketing director for hip reconstruction; Brad Tandy, assistant general counsel and corporate compliance officer; Mark Vandewalle, director of engineering services; John Wagoner, director of regulatory affairs compliance; Tim Weis, distributor; Darlene Whaley, vice president of human resources; John White, director of patient-matched implants; Rex White, director of quality assurance; Jack Wilhite, process engineer; Dan Williamson, director of business development; and Lonnie Witham, senior regulatory affairs specialist.

Many outside Biomet also shed light on the company's history: John Cuckler, M.D.; Berkley Duck, attorney; Henry Finn, M.D.; William Head, M.D.; Miles Igo, early investor; Adolph Lombardi, M.D.; Tom Mallory, M.D.; John Repicci, D.D.S., M.D.; and Merrill Ritter, M.D.

As always, special thanks are extended to the dedicated staff at Write Stuff Enterprises. Copyeditor Bonnie Freeman and transcriptionist Mary Aaron worked quickly and efficiently. Indexer Erica Orloff assembled the comprehensive index. Particular gratitude is also due to Jon VanZile, executive editor; Melody Maysonet, senior editor; Heather Deeley, assistant editor; and Heather G. Cohn, former associate editor; Sandy Cruz, senior art director; Rachelle Donley, Wendy Iverson, and Dennis Shockley, art directors; Bruce Borich, production manager; Marianne Roberts, vice president of administration; Linda Edell, executive assistant to Jeffrey L. Rodengen; Monica Kjeldgaard, former executive assistant to Jeffrey L. Rodengen; Lars Jessen, director of marketing; Sheryl Herdsman, former director of marketing; Grace Kurotori, former sales and promotions manager; Nina Burrows, former accounting assistant; Rory Schmer, distribution supervisor; Jennifer Walter, administrative assistant; and David Patten, former executive author.

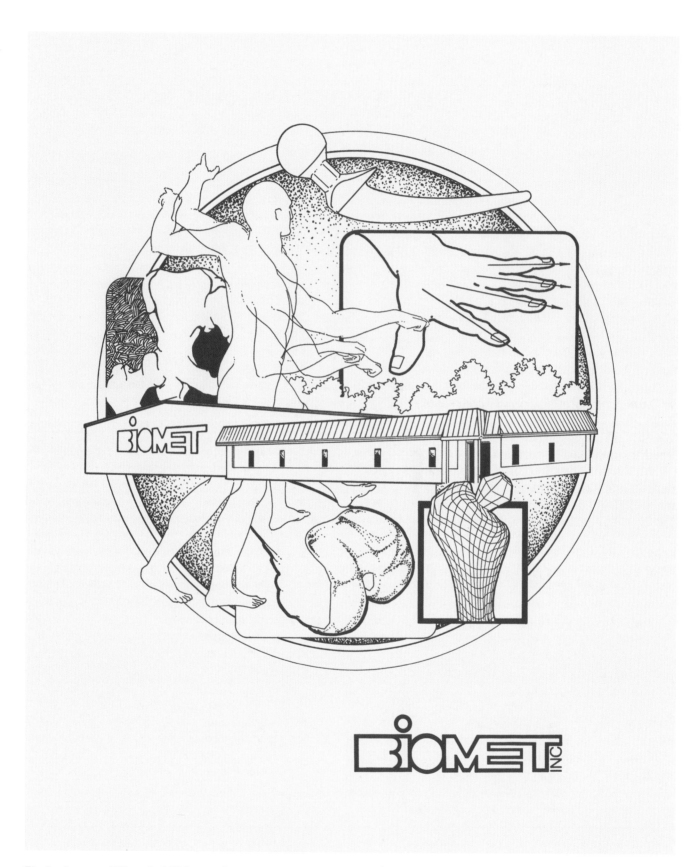

The back cover of Biomet's 1981 annual report, which forecast sales of $36.7 million by the end of 1985, a five-year forecast that would prove remarkably close.

CHAPTER ONE

CONVERGING FORCES

1975–1981

Basically, we take anatomical structures that were designed a long time ago by God and try to make metal or plastic implants that work.

—Dane A. Miller, Ph.D., president and CEO, Biomet, 2001

IN SEPTEMBER 1975 COWORKERS Dane A. Miller and Jerry L. Ferguson went sailing. By the time their boat returned to shore, the idea that triggered Biomet had been born.[1]

Miller was the director of development engineering and custom products for Zimmer USA, a leading producer of orthopedic surgical implants based in Warsaw, Indiana, and a division of Bristol-Myers. He had earned a B.S. in mechanical materials science engineering from the General Motors Institute (now Kettering University), as well as an M.S. and a Ph.D. in materials science biomedical engineering from the University of Cincinnati.[2]

Ferguson, with a B.S. in marketing from Ball State University, was Zimmer's group product director for surgical implants.[3]

Miller and Ferguson's dream of launching a new business was put on hold, however, as each confronted other challenges. Miller moved to San Diego, California, to become the director of biomedical engineering for Cutter Biomedical, a division of Cutter Laboratories.[4] Ferguson joined Orthopedic Equipment Company (OEC), in Bourbon, Indiana, as director of marketing.[5]

Yet both men held on to their dream. Early in 1977 Ferguson contacted Miller and rekindled the discussion they had begun more than a year before.[6] Later that year they joined forces with two other OEC

executives: Niles L. Noblitt, director of technical services and an engineer with experience in developmental and federal regulatory affairs, and M. Ray Harroff, OEC's product manager.[7]

"Jerry had the plan all put together, and it was a beautiful thing," Harroff said. "It was a pretty good blend of personalities and people."[8]

Opportunities in Orthopedics

Launching an orthopedic company was anything but easy. Dr. Tom Mallory, a Harvard-educated physician who would later develop implants with Biomet, remembered his surprise upon hearing that a new orthopedic company was being launched.

I happened upon Dane Miller at an industry meeting, and he said he and three friends had formed their own company.

I thought how crazy that was because I couldn't imagine why someone with a Ph.D. who had secured [jobs with Zimmer and Cutter] as an

Dane Miller (left) and Niles Noblitt would still play key operational roles in the company beyond the millennium as president-CEO and chairman of the board, respectively.

The four founders and their wives set out on an exciting adventure when they started Biomet in 1977. From left are Mary Louise and Dane Miller, Nancy and Niles Noblitt, Norma and Jerry Ferguson, and Rose and Ray Harroff in Washington, D.C., celebrating their Entrepreneurial Success Award in 1991.

engineer would venture off into a very difficult and competitive arena. But Miller is a true entrepreneur in the great American spirit.[9]

All four founders and their wives were aware of the risk involved, but perhaps not the depth of that risk. "We were young," Mary Louise Miller said. "We were naive. We had great hopes for lots of things."[10]

Nancy Noblitt remembers it as an exciting time. "Niles was real gung ho and it sounded very doable," she said. "We had only one child then, and we thought, '[We] can always go back to whatever [we] did before' if we had to."[11]

The risky venture was complicated not only by the formidable competition of firmly established leaders like Zimmer, but by government involvement. Until the mid-1970s, the orthopedic and medical device industry acted without much government regulation or oversight. In 1976, however, that changed dramatically. That year, the development, testing, marketing, and manufacturing of all medical devices— such as arthroscopic, reconstructive, spinal, and internal fixation devices, fracture healing, bone cements, and bone substitute materials— became regulated under the Medical Device

Amendments to the Federal Food, Drug and Cosmetic Act.[12]

In an attempt to ensure safety and effectiveness, the 1976 amendments forced medical device manufacturers to comply with strict regulations governing labeling, quality assurance, manufacturing practices, and clinical investigations involving humans. In addition, new product safety regulations controlled the sales and marketing of all such devices.[13]

"The feeling was that the new regulations had created a substantial barrier to entry for new companies and that it would be extremely risky and expensive for a new player to try to enter the market," Miller said.[14]

Instead of seeing the amendments as a barrier, however, Biomet recognized it could actually gain from them. The company's founders simply built the company around the new regulations. "We didn't have a lot of historic product and process skeletons in the closet; we could start anew and (perhaps) even take advantage of the fact that our competition was going to have to change the way they did things," Miller said.[15]

Essentially, the Biomet group thought they could take suggestions from orthopedic surgeons and come out with improved implants faster than their large competitors could.[16]

"The basic concept of what we do is fairly simple," said Mark Vandewalle, director of engineering services, "and that is trying to improve the outcomes, trying to identify what the surgeons' and patients' needs are, and addressing them in a safe manner."[17]

"Our goal," Miller agreed, "was to become the most responsive company in orthopedics while simultaneously providing patients with the highest quality and most clinically proven products in the marketplace."[18]

In the late 1970s, it was a goal that many other industry executives thought impossible to achieve.[19] "I was one of the guys across town who was saying 'This little company can't be a player,'" said Vice President of Sales Dave Montgomery, who worked at Zimmer for 10 years before joining the Biomet force. "Fortunately, I was smart enough along the way to change my mind."[20]

A New Name in Orthopedics

The four men initially decided to name their company "Biomed," but an agricultural chemical company based in Georgia had already coined the word. At Ferguson's suggestion, the company, on November 30, 1977, became Biomet—bio for body and met for metallurgical implants.[21]

In January 1978, the young but seasoned executives made their dream reality. Noblitt, 27, Miller, 31, Ferguson, 38, and Harroff, 39, quit their jobs and went into business together, with the help

of their wives, in a converted barn on State Road 15, south of Warsaw, Indiana.[22] With more than 10 years of experience, Rose Harroff became the original director of soft goods manufacturing. Nancy Noblitt worked as Niles's secretary and kept the distribution and quality control records. Norma Ferguson and Mary Louise Miller performed a variety of clerical duties.

"We all went to work," Norma Ferguson said. "[We] decided early on [that] if the husbands were going to spend long, 12-hour days [at Biomet], the wives would work too. Really, all along, we talked about this as an adventure."[23]

The Harroffs' children were teenagers, which enabled Rose to work full-time. The other three wives, however, had small children to tend to, recalled Mary Louise Miller.

[The men] were very insistent that we were always home when the children got out of school, and that worked well because we would go in in the morning, when they were in school, and come home when they came home from school. Oftentimes, we'd have to go back to work, and we'd take our children with us, and that was just our life. All we did was Biomet. All four couples worked really well together, and it was a big family project.[24]

Nancy, Mary Louise, and Norma took turns sorting the mail and posting the bills. Even the

Right: Jerry Ferguson, Biomet's vice chairman, first envisioned Biomet in 1975 while sailing with Dane Miller.

Far right: Ray Harroff, one of the four founders of Biomet, retired from company operations but kept a seat on the board.

THE HISTORY OF ORTHOPEDICS

ORTHOPEDIC SURGERY IS THE MEDIcal specialty pertaining to the care of the musculoskeletal system, meaning the bones, joints, muscles, tendons, and ligaments of the arms, legs, and spine, along with the spinal and peripheral nerves that carry signals to and from these tissues.

Evidence suggests that basic orthopedic practices have existed since ancient times. Mummified bodies, wall paintings, and hieroglyphics have shown that the early Egyptians suffered from the same problems we experience today. Splints of bamboo, reeds, wood, or bark padded with linen have been found on mummies. There is also evidence of crutches, the earliest known record coming from a carving made in 2830 B.C. on a portal of King Hirkouf's tomb.[1]

The modern roots of this medical specialty can be traced to 1741 and the Parisian publication of a book by Nicolas Andry (1658–1742) translated into English in 1943 as *Orthopaedia: or the Art of Correcting and Preventing Deformities in Children.* Andry derived the

word *orthopedie* from the Greek words *ortho* (straight) and *ped* (child).[2]

Consequently, in the 18th and 19th centuries, orthopedists were devoted largely to the care of children with spine and limb deformities. Early orthopedists often used braces or other treatments to make the child "straight." Today, however, orthopedic surgeons care for patients of all ages—from newborns with clubfoot, to young athletes requiring arthroscopic surgery, to people with arthritis who need joint replacements.[3]

One of the most common joint replacements performed today involves the hip, which is essentially a ball-and-socket joint. The hip joint is located where the upper end of the femur meets the acetabulum. The femur, or thighbone, looks like a long stem with a ball on the end. The acetabulum is a socket, or cuplike cavity, in the pelvis, or hipbone.[4] It is a very stable joint because of the deep socket, which limits hip motion. The most common clinical conditions involving the hip include osteo- or rheumatoid arthritis, fracture, and dislocation.[5]

During a hip replacement, a surgeon removes deteriorated bone tissue and cartilage from the hip joint. The healthy parts of the hip are left intact. Then the surgeon replaces the head of the femur (the ball) and the acetabulum (the socket) with new, artificial parts made of materials that allow a natural, gliding motion of the joint.[6]

Sometimes surgeons use a special cement to anchor the new parts of the hip joint to the existing, healthy bone. This cement is a type of "grout," or filler, and this method is often referred to as a cemented procedure. In an

---

The device at the top of the photo is an original hip designed by pioneer Sir John Charnley. Below it is Biomet's porous-coated Mallory-Head hip and Bi-Metric femoral components.

uncemented procedure, the artificial parts are coated with porous material that allows the patient's bone to grow into the pores and hold the new parts in place. Some surgeons use a hybrid replacement, which consists of a cemented femur and an uncemented acetabular part, or vice versa.[7]

The history of hip replacement surgery dates back to the 1800s, when surgeons used prostheses of various materials, including an all-metal hip secured with metal screws. In 1890, an ivory ball was placed onto the neck of the femur and was held in place with screws and a type of bone glue. There were problems with erosion and loosening, however.[8]

The next big advance came in 1938, when British surgeon John Wiles performed the first hip replacement operation using stainless steel for the head of the joint.[9]

However, hip arthroplasty, or reconstruction surgery, was not truly successful until 1958, when Sir John Charnley, a British surgeon and bioengineer, introduced the concept of using high-density polyethylene, or plastic, as an articulating material with a stainless steel femoral head. Both components were held in place with methylmethacrylate, or plastic, cement.[10] (Incidentally, knee replacement surgery developed directly out of Charnley's work on the artificial hip.)[11]

Total hip replacement operations have been performed in the United States since 1970, and the surgery is still based on Charnley's concept.

According to the American Academy of Orthopaedic Surgeons, approximately 168,000 total hip replacement operations were performed in the United States in 2001, and fewer than 10 percent required further surgery. New technology, such as that advanced by Biomet, and improvements in surgical techniques, have greatly reduced the risks involved with hip replacements.[12]

Noblitts' daughter, Sarah, pitched in—as an 18-month-old model in the first Biomet catalog. "She did not enjoy that," Nancy Noblitt recalled.[25]

Walter P. Spires Jr. was the first professional employee to be "hired," said Niles Noblitt. "He was a biomedical engineer with a master's degree, but he did what the rest of us did: he cleaned parts, whatever was necessary to take care of the customer."[26]

With $110,000 of their own money, the couples sought out the help of investor Miles Igo, a man with a small orthopedic company called Warsaw Orthopedic, valuable contacts, and a Small Business Administration (SBA) loan.

Igo helped secure an SBA loan for Biomet and became an initial shareholder of the company. Approximately two years later, the other shareholders acquired Igo's ownership.[27]

"It was a very risky venture," Igo said. "I was sweating a little bit. I felt they were going too fast for me when I had so much on the line, and Warsaw Orthopedic was in debt—I was worried about everybody going broke. So I took Warsaw Orthopedic and went on.

"They're great people," Igo added. "They're just fantastic gentlemen, and I felt very lucky the way it's turned out—to even be associated with them."[28]

Igo's investment and contacts came along at a crucial time for the founders of the fledgling company. Not only did Igo help them obtain a $500,000 SBA loan and an additional $100,000 line of bank credit, but he also supplied Biomet with a temporary facility.

"We rented space from Miles for our office and shipping facilities," Harroff said of Biomet's first shop. "We bought [soft goods from his company] and shipped [them] to our customers, trying to establish our customer base."[29]

Harroff recalled being the first to arrive each morning.

It was a struggle. Everybody was working 12 to 16 hours a day, including weekends. I'd come in and they didn't have any lights on and I kind of [felt] my way around. One morning, I stumbled over a guy [who worked for Warsaw Orthopedic] that was sleeping. This guy obviously had decided not to go home the night before and was lying there on the floor. It scared both of us to death.[30]

THE NEWEST MANUFACTURER OF ORTHOPEDIC IMPLANTS AND SOFT GOODS IS WORKING NEARLY AROUND THE CLOCK ....

..... **THAT'S WHY THE LIGHTS ARE STILL ON.**

BIOMET INC · P.O. BOX 587 · WARSAW, INDIANA 46580

Biomet's first color print advertisement, a six-page ad, appeared in 1978.

Their first attempts to raise money after Igo left, however, were not so rewarding. Miller recalled that venture capital was not the household word it would later become.

Now, everybody seems to know what venture capital is, and most people don't remember when venture capital had a limited source. The only venture capital firm we knew of in the Midwest was Continental Venture Capital, and in fact our first effort was to meet with them and try to convince them that they ought to invest $500,000 in the company.

We made a trip to Chicago and sat down with a couple of individuals whose names I don't even recollect today. They took us to lunch in the executive cafeteria at Continental Bank in Chicago

and proceeded to explain to us how important Harvard MBAs were and that each of them was a Harvard MBA and that we ought to go back to Indiana and milk the cows. A couple of years later, Continental Bank went bankrupt, if you remember.[31]

Blood, Sweat, and Cows

As Niles Noblitt said, the good old days were not always good. The men struggled through the first two years, nearly folding more than once.

"We actually began operations in 1978," said Jerry Ferguson, who now serves as vice chairman of the board. "I'm not sure when the money ran out, but it ran out fairly quickly. The four of us established our salaries in '78 at $17,000 a year, and I think it was maybe three or four months later that we dropped [them] to $12,000. So we were eating a lot of spaghetti, a lot of hamburger."[32]

In fact, in an effort to feed their families, the founders bought three calves to graze on the overgrown grass behind the shop. The men planned to fatten the calves over the summer and fall and then slaughter them in the winter.[33]

"Well, they were all heifers apparently," Ferguson said. "What we didn't count on was the heifers going into heat, and each time they did, they would chase the trains. I don't know how many times we actually had to go retrieve those calves from the neighbors' yards. They weren't putting any fat on. So when they were slaughtered, the meat was by no means prime quality. Some of the kids wouldn't eat the meat because they had named [the calves]."[34]

Nancy Noblitt recalled taking her daughters to visit the cows. "It was very hard when we butchered [them]," she said. "We didn't really want to eat [them]."[35]

But survival was foremost on their minds, and each day was a challenge, Harroff said.

"I know Dane used to sit with the president of one of the local banks, and all the money the bank would give us was based on the invoices that we would present them," he said. "So Dane would sit down with the banker every Friday afternoon to determine how much funding they'd be able to give us. Dane would have a stack of invoices, maybe a half inch to an inch thick, and they'd go through those one by one. I'm not too sure that Dane wasn't taking the top one and putting it on the bottom until he got enough money to make it through the next week," Harroff laughed.[36]

Biomet soon outgrew the tiny office, so a gutted mobile home was attached to a hole cut in the wall. The mobile home was used to house finished goods and shipping.[37]

Charles Niemier, as a field auditor for the accounting firm Coopers and Lybrand, worked through the summer of 1980 auditing Biomet's books.

When I first met the founders, they were operating a small sweatshop. Sweatshop is a good description because they were living hand-to-mouth trying to pay their bills and wouldn't turn the air-conditioning on until late in the afternoon.

All their books and records were in shoe boxes. They didn't have enough room, so they brought a card table from home, and I worked in a corner. By 2 o'clock in the afternoon, it was so darn hot in there and I had sweat dripping off my nose onto my work papers. But there was this electricity in the air that you could feel every day. It was incredible. Here were a bunch of guys [who] had a dream, and you could just sense the desire to work toward the dream. Coupled with that was their intense desire to survive.[38]

Realizing how badly Biomet needed its financial matters looked after, Miller asked Niemier to join the team.

"It was my job to figure out who got paid when," Niemier said. "When the phone rang, [the office] was so small that it rang through the whole place, and I would just cringe, thinking, 'Oh God, this is somebody else looking for their money.'"[39]

In those days Biomet relied heavily upon checks from orthopedic surgeon Dr. Merrill Ritter, one of the company's earliest accounts. "There were times that I funded [projects] simply because of my belief in Dane Miller," Ritter said. "He's an honest man and an ethical person, and that's someone you can put everything into."[40]

"He was our first what you call big homerun hitter that we were ever associated with," Harroff recalled.[41] In fact, Niemier relied heavily on Dr. Ritter.

Merrill Ritter believed in us. On Friday, I'd pass payroll out to our 25 to 30 team members. On Saturday morning, my wife and I would go to the post office to see if [Dr. Ritter's] check came in from his hospital, because that's how we covered payroll.[42]

Niemier had two assistants upon joining the Biomet team: Mary Louise Miller and Norma Ferguson.

"We thought it would be better if we didn't work for our own husbands," Norma Ferguson laughed. "We're still married today, so I guess it was a good idea."[43]

Unable to afford an office cleaning staff, the company relied on the women to share those responsibilities. "The night before I delivered our second child, Catherine, I was in Niles's office, cleaning," recalled Nancy Noblitt.[44]

Cleaning the office was only half the battle. "Niles used to cure molds of epoxy or a prototype hip in our oven at home," recalled his wife.[45] Strange smells filled the air in those early days.

Into Manufacturing

In the beginning, the founders intended Biomet to be a marketing and development company that would contract with independent job shops to manufacture Biomet-designed implants.

"Our original plan to rely on local suppliers wasn't working," however, Niles Noblitt said. "We needed rapid turnaround of new products and product supply that we could get only if we had internal control of the development and production cycle."[46]

The founders discovered early on that subcontract manufacture was unreliable, Ferguson agreed. "Nobody could meet specs. Nobody met time constraints. And pricing was out of our control."[47]

Miller gave additional reasons for Biomet's expansion into manufacturing. "We found out we were teaching [the job-shop owners] how to make our products to sell to our competition," Miller explained. "So we began making soft goods [such as arm slings, knee immobilizers, and rib belts] and our own implants to protect our implant technology."[48]

Dan Cordill, senior manufacturing engineer of replacement hips today, was one of the first machinists hired by Biomet. He had taken the helm of his small, family-owned machine shop at the age of 20, when his father died. Soon afterward, the Cordills sold their equipment to Biomet, and Cordill went to work for OEC in 1980.[49]

"About a month later I got a call from Dane," Cordill recalled. "Their two machinists were having a difficult time running the equipment Biomet had purchased off of us, which obviously I knew all the intricacies of. So they offered me a job, which I accepted."[50]

Generating Confidence

Soft goods were the key to getting Biomet's foot in the orthopedic manufacturing door, Harroff explained. They were "a lot less expensive [to make] than implants, which would require really expensive machinery. So that was the main reason Rose and I were both involved—because of the products we were going to start the company with."[51] Both Ray and Rose Harroff were experts

Above: A sign marks the construction site of Biomet's first corporate headquarters, begun in April 1980.

Below: Before the construction of the manufacturing plant, Biomet operated out of this converted barn, approximately 3.5 miles south of Warsaw, Indiana, on State Road 15.

in the soft-goods business. Rose had been a manager and Ray a product manager at OEC.

Soft goods were "low-market-entry products from both a technology and a manufacturing-cost point of view," Miller said. "No orthopedic surgeon is going to be uncomfortable giving his patient an arm sling or cervical collar made by a new company. We felt it was important to get our boxes and our name on the shelf."[52]

Noblitt recalled that early strategy. "If we were going to sell surgeons our implants, we were going to have to earn their business first."[53] But all four founders and their wives agreed that the reliance on soft goods was a short-term strategy and that the company needed to be a full-line orthopedic company eventually in order to compete.

It was not uncommon for the wives of the four Biomet founders to be seen working on soft goods in the sewing department in the State Road 15 facility.[54] That dedication was clear in Biomet's first color print advertisement, which announced, "The Newest Manufacturer of Orthopedic

Implants and Soft Goods Is Working Nearly around the Clock. . . . That's Why the Lights Are Still On."[55]

"It was a real family environment," said Garry England, senior vice president of Warsaw operations. "We would have carry-in lunches, and you knew everybody's first name, their wives' names, and how many kids they had. The ladies in the sewing department would bring in these wonderful dishes on holidays, and we'd eat like kings. It was great."[56]

At the same time Biomet launched its soft-goods line, the company was developing its other lines, which included reconstructive products for the hip and knee, internal fixation products such as hip plates and bone screws, and a closed-wound suction device. These products were as important for attracting experienced distribution as they were for their direct sales.[57]

Biomet entered the implant market by redesigning existing implants, such as the total hip and total knee products. "The objective was to update those products and make them stronger, do a variety of [research and development] designs, and see to it that the product would last longer, create less stress, and be less painful than the competitors'," Ferguson said. "And we were successful in doing that."[58]

One of the very first implantable products designed by Biomet was the Concentric Hex, a unique compression screw used as a healing aid for hip fractures. It was based on an item produced by a competitor and offered improved design features.[59]

"It was a novel approach to fixing hip fractures," Miller said. "We brought that product to market in late 1978 and continue to sell it today."[60]

Biomet's first line of prostheses, however, was for the femur, or thighbone, and total-hip-replacement market. The firm began concentrating on artificial hips in mid-1978, focusing on the titanium-6 aluminum-4 vanadium alloy and a porous coating for the new alloy.[61]

Right: The Concentric Hex Hip Screw, a fixation device for stabilizing fractures

Below: An enlargement of a microscopic photograph of porous titanium alloy coating, one of the core technologies used by Biomet. The coating encourages a strong bond to form between the implant and new bone growth.

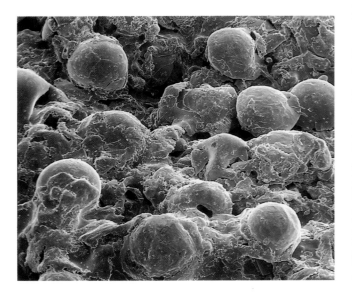

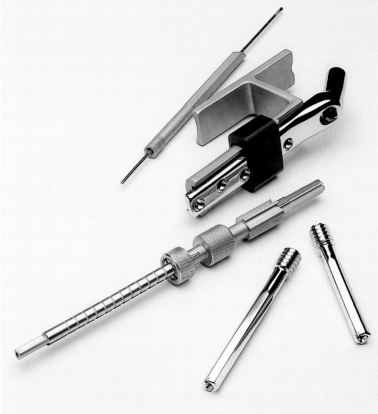

KEEPING IT IN THE FAMILY

DANE MILLER IS A WALKING EXPERI-ment—his own guinea pig, if you will. But perhaps nothing less than first-hand experience could give someone the confidence to implant his company's first hip into his grandmother.

By the time Grace Shumaker received Biomet's first implant—made of titanium—in 1978, Miller had been carrying a piece of the metal under the skin of his forearm for five years.[1]

"I was pushing for titanium while the rest of the industry had already kind of turned its back on it and walked away," Miller said. "It was used in a lot of our implant products, which most of our competitors found fault with and then later copied."[2]

It was Miller's adamant belief in titanium as the most biocompatible metal available for surgical implant devices that led him to do the personal research.

Grace Shumaker, the grandmother of Biomet CEO Dane Miller, was the recipient of the company's first hip implant.

I believe it was in 1974. We had had a tornado go through the county and [we] didn't have any electricity in Warsaw. So I called a friend who was an orthopedic surgeon and said, 'I've got a [titanium] sample that we made for rabbit testing. Would you mind putting a piece in my arm?' Sounds a little goofy, but I had nothing better to do that day.

So I was comfortable with the material, confident in the design, and had no apprehension whatsoever about the first Biomet total joint product going in my grandmother.[3]

Miller was convinced that over time the characteristics of titanium would not change. According to a history of Biomet's early years, Miller decided to have the titanium surgically removed nearly nine years later and to personally test a new wound closure product called Dermizip.

The outcome: Numerous histology and biocompatibility tests performed on the removed titanium proved exactly what Dane predicted—metallurgically, the titanium came

---

Dane Miller recalled the reasoning behind the development of plasma spray coating, spearheaded by Niles Noblitt.

We knew we wanted to process a coating using titanium because of its mechanical properties and biocompatibility, but we wanted to put a porous coating on it so you could implant a [device] without having to cement it in the bone.

Plasma spray coating technology had originally been developed for a different application. It had historically been used as an economical way to address the problem of worn shafts and bearing surfaces such as in locomotive engines. A dense metal material was applied to resurface

the worn part and then it was remachined to match its original dimensions. Biomet began utilizing this technology to apply a highly porous metal to surfaces of implants so bone could grow into it.[62]

Used earlier in cardiovascular implants,[63] plasma spray coating would become one of the core technology platforms separating Biomet from its competition.

In keeping with the family spirit that characterized the company, the recipient of Biomet's first hip implant in 1978 was Miller's grandmother, Grace Shumaker.[64]

At the end of 1978, Biomet had recorded sales of $17,000 and a loss of $63,000.[65] Clearly, launch-out exactly as it went in.[4] The histology around the implant was flawless.[5] But Miller's legendary in-house success with titanium may forever be tied to the legendary in-house failure of Dermizip. Ironically, it was considered the firm's most promising product at the time.[6]

This revolutionary product was to catapult Biomet into the surgical-wound-closure market. Dermizip, a device produced from polyethylene and stainless steel, was intended to compete with conventional sutures and staples. It was to offer speed and precision to the surgeon and better promote the natural wound-healing process with improved cosmetic results.[7]

However, things didn't work out that way. Dermizip never formally went to market, and in-house, it became known as dermiscar.[8]

Miller was again the guinea pig when the first Dermizip application broke down and the attachment apparatus (identical pin harness) would not hold. Not one to give up easily, Miller met up with the doctor who designed Dermizip, John Sheehan, at O'Hare Airport. In an airport hallway, Dr. Sheehan replaced the original unit and Miller flew off to Europe. Ten more days passed, and when healing still had not taken place, Miller had the Dermizip unit removed while in Sweden.[9]

"Just to listen to it, it sounded like the most ingenious thing you ever heard of," said fellow Biomet founder M. Ray Harroff. "It was going to be a wound closure device that worked like a zipper.

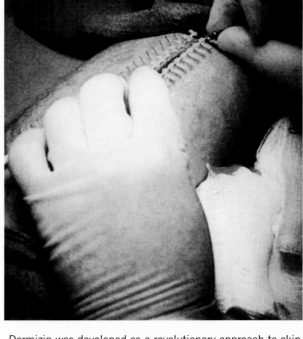

Dermizip was developed as a revolutionary approach to skin closure. It promoted the natural healing process, but scarring made the innovative product unattractive, and it never formally went to market.

"One of the big advantages of the Dermizip was going to be that there would be less scarring, but it actually turned out to [scar] as much or more," Harroff said.[10]

ing a new orthopedics company wasn't going to be easy. By early 1979, most of the initial investment capital was gone, including the $500,000 SBA-guaranteed loan.[66]

Sources and Resources

"We were basically out of money," Dane Miller said. "Many weeks, we weren't cashing our payroll checks because the company didn't have the money in the bank. The founders kind of took it on the chin financially."[67]

Mary Louise recalled the first American Academy of Orthopaedic Surgeons annual meeting she attended with Biomet.

Biomet was very poor at that time. We didn't really have enough money to entertain our doctors properly. So I made food at home, froze it, and put it in the suitcase.

The first night we were there, we ordered a lot of food brought in on silver trays. Then I put the silver trays under my bed, and when [housekeeping] would come the next day, my husband was always "asleep."

I used those silver trays for the three nights we were there and tried to make the food look like we had ordered it.[68]

Miller and the others began to have their doubts about whether they could raise sufficient capital to stay in the business, let alone become full-fledged manufacturers. They even considered selling out.[69] Then Miller and Ferguson met Kenneth and Jerry Miller (no relation to Dane), brothers and attorneys from Kalamazoo, Michigan, who were on the lookout for investment opportunities.

Biomet's first presentation to the Miller brothers met with a refusal.

"Ferguson and Dane got in their car, drove up here, and wouldn't take no for an answer," Jerry Miller recalled. "We'll forever be grateful to them for that."[70]

"Dane is a very persuasive individual," Harroff said. "I don't know if [the Miller brothers] had the foresight to really see what the potential was, or if it was just Dane's persuasiveness."[71]

The Biomet founders brought back a check for $50,000, which was 10 percent of the Millers' investment, Ferguson said. "The dollars were dwindling, and $500,000 was what we needed to keep going. As I recall, that $50,000 was consumed probably in a week, maybe less."[72]

In the end, the Miller brothers were impressed with the company founders and their business plan. Their $500,000 bought a one-third equity position in Biomet, and the brothers still serve on Biomet's board of directors.[73]

"We were novice investors," Jerry Miller said. "If we were any better investors, we probably wouldn't have done the deal or done it as well. Our investment in Biomet wasn't done with intellect as much as with luck."[74]

Although the Miller brothers' investment enabled Biomet's founders to avoid selling the company, they take little credit for its success.

"What we invested in was the four founders," Kenneth Miller said. "If they were out building shopping malls, we would have invested in the four of them anyway."[75]

The year 1979 also saw the introduction of Biomet's Total Cruciate Condylar Knee System (predecessor to the AGC Total Knee System), which incorporated the company's first compression-molded tibial component.[76] The compression molding was a proprietary process that involved molding ultra-high-molecular-weight polyethylene powder under heat and pressure to produce a finished part. The part was then trimmed, cleaned, packaged, and sterilized.[77]

By the time Biomet closed its books for 1979, its second full year in business, sales had reached $517,000—$500,000 more than its first year.

Corporate Headquarters

To accommodate its growth, on April 1, 1980, Biomet broke ground at the Warsaw Airport Industrial Park for the first stage of its 23,000-square-foot corporate headquarters. Funding

Brothers Jerry (left) and Kenneth Miller (right), no relation to Dane Miller, took a chance as novice investors when they put $500,000 into Biomet in 1979. The deal saved Biomet from bankruptcy and initiated a lasting rapport between the Miller brothers and Biomet's four founders.

for the new facility was obtained through a combination of corporate funds and the sale of economic development revenue bonds.[78]

By August 1980 the first phase was completed, allowing Biomet to move its manufacturing office and storage space under one roof and to vacate its three independent locations: the State Road 15 building that housed Biomet's sewing operation, shipping, and administration; a U-Store-It warehouse on Winona Avenue, used to store soft-good raw materials; and a small metal-manu-facturing operation located in Warsaw's Acme Building.[79]

At the end of 1980, Biomet's sales had climbed past the $1 million mark to $1.07 million.[80] Key to Biomet's growing success was the influence of local, independent distributors that served as Biomet's main contact with surgeons.[81]

As Miller noted, "We were able to find distributors that, for one reason or another, had discontinued relationships with our competitors but had contacts in the market and knowledge of the product lines."[82] In fact, Biomet's first 50 distributors either had worked for other orthopedic companies or had extensive experience in the field.[83]

However, getting experienced distributors to sign on with an upstart company like Biomet was a sizable challenge. Accordingly, Biomet treated distributors as important customers, responding to their needs for product development and supply. In short, distributors were part of the "team."

Tim L. Weis remembered leaving a comfortable position with a competitor to take a chance on Biomet in 1980.

I walked in, and there were these four guys' wives at sewing machines making soft goods, cleaning up, doing clerical duties, and the rest of the guys buzzing around. Their little trailer that they had pulled up to the shipping department had two rows in it, and a very, very, very skinny individual who could get between those two rows was doing the shipping, and I thought, "My God, what have I done."[84]

Left: The Total Cruciate Condylar Knee System provides the necessary components for the reconstruction of the knee's three articular surfaces.

Below: Tim Weis left a comfortable position with a competitor to take a chance on Biomet in 1980. He was one of the company's first distributors and would remain a team member into the new millennium.

As for the distributors who turned down the founders, Weis recalled the words of Jerry Ferguson.

He said to me, "You know what? The heck with these guys. So what. If you lose your house, you can live in a trailer for a while." I thought, "Boy, they are serious people."

That stayed with me because when I saw these families and knew that they were willing to live in trailers to keep this thing going, I wanted to be part of that, and now I feel very, very fortunate that I was able to hook on with Biomet early enough. I always joked to Jerry that the guys [who] turned them down probably can't find a building tall enough to jump off.[85]

Dane Miller recognized that it would be difficult to talk a sales rep into working for Biomet, a company with a limited product offering in those early days. "It would also take another leap of faith for an orthopedic surgeon to be convinced that we could, in fact, develop and produce high-quality products that would serve patients well," Miller said.[86]

"Obviously, the distributors did a fantastic job for us," said Ray Harroff, who has since retired. "They led us in the right direction as far as determining which total joints we should be getting involved with. So we started developing total joints along their recommendations."[87]

Biomet also benefited from fortunate timing. The company's early years coincided with a tremendous boom in demand for orthopedic implants.

As Miller explained, "In the early 1970s, the rule of thumb was you didn't put a hip in a patient until he was old enough that the hip would last" his or her remaining lifetime. This

A circa 1980 advertisement for Biomet's September Specials displays products crucial to Biomet's foundation. Soft goods such as these were the key to getting Biomet's foot in the orthopedic manufacturing door. They required sewing machines rather than expensive machinery, and they did not necessitate approval from the Food and Drug Administration.

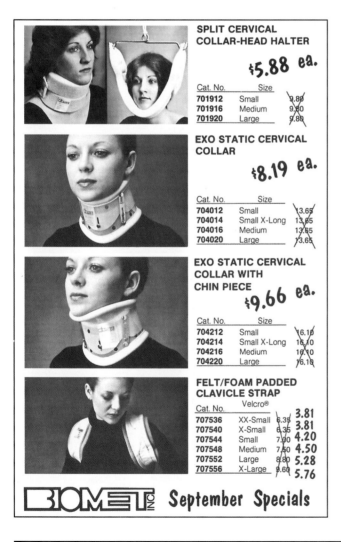

concern all but excluded operating on patients younger than 60 or 65. But in the early 1980s, due to new implant designs and a more aggressive clinical protocol, many orthopedic surgeons began to change their traditional thinking about suitable candidates.[88]

Over time, surgeons became more confident that a total joint implant would last in younger patients as well. Consequently, implant operations jumped from approximately 10,000 worldwide annually in the early 1980s to more than 400,000 annually in the United States alone during the late 1990s.[89]

In an effort to fortify its long-term financial position and allow for continuing growth, Biomet raised $1.25 million through the sale of subordinated debentures on May 1, 1981.[90]

The Expanding Product Line

By the end of 1981, Biomet's growing product lines had fused into five groups:

1. Reconstructive Devices consisted of implants for hip and knee replacement as well as many instruments used to perform such surgeries. Within this category, in March 1981 Biomet introduced a new acetabular cup designed to be used with the company's femoral components, which included a titanium alloy reinforcing shell and integral bone cement spacing pegs. Trade-named the Bio-Clad Acetabular Cup, it addressed the long-term clinical problems associated with earlier acetabular cups' loosening.[91]
2. Internal Fixation Devices, such as Biomet's Concentric Hex hip fixation system, were used by orthopedic surgeons to set fractures accurately and as an aid in trauma surgery. Such implants were intended not to replace normal body structures but to aid in healing. These implants could be removed when healing was complete.[92]
3. Orthopedic Support Products included most of the standard products used by orthopedists, including cervical collars; clavicle supports; slings, splints, and

other immobilizers; wrist and forearm supports; rib belts; abdominal and sacral supports; traction belts; and other miscellaneous devices.[93]

4. Operating Room Supplies consisted of one principal product: Biomet's closed-wound suction system, used for postoperative fluid removal.[94]

5. Custom or Specialty Products provided unique orthopedic devices for unusual orthopedic problems.[95]

Biomet's sales in 1981 grew to $2.02 million—an 89 percent increase from 1980. That represented a gross profit of $1.1 million and generated net income of $213,222—a welcome 1,233 percent increase from 1980.[96]

As noted in Biomet's 1981 annual report, the sizable increase in net income "resulted principally from the distribution of fixed manufacturing overhead costs over the substantially higher sales level for the most recent year." The jump was also due to the increase in the percentage of goods manufactured exclusively in-house, which reduced the overall cost of goods sold.[97]

The combination of a responsive sales force and innovative and sophisticated orthopedic products primed Biomet for a future of rising profits.

The APF and Mosc 28 hip systems helped drive sales in Biomet's flourishing reconstructive products category.

CHAPTER TWO

A BOLD MOVE PAYS OFF

1981–1986

I believe as we look back 10 years, the evolution of orthopedics has led to the rehabilitation of America.

—Dane A. Miller, Ph.D., president and CEO, 2001

BY THE EARLY 1980S, BIOMET was burning through cash at a rapid pace. In only four years, sales had gone from zero to $2.02 million. The company had built its headquarters in Warsaw and rapidly expanded its sales force.

To finance this growth, in 1981 Biomet issued debenture bonds with attached warrants. This kind of corporate bond allowed holders to exercise the warrant at a later date, meaning they could buy stock at a predetermined price. The bond sale was offered through Traub and Company.

Jerry Ferguson, who traveled with Dane Miller to promote the bond sale, remembered their road show as an exercise in frugality.

"Traub and Company did not supply anyone," Ferguson said.

It was just Dane and I, and we were frugal in those days. I remember we spent the night in the motor home at the Presbyterian church somewhere in Cincinnati. Dane forgot to turn on the generator, so the next morning, the water was cold for the showers.[1]

While Miller admitted later that the cold water was another deliberate money-saving technique, cold showers weren't the only challenge. Without representatives from Traub and Company, Miller

and Ferguson were left to explain the concept of bonds with attached warrants to potential investors. Having degrees in engineering and marketing, they realized they needed a quick financial education.

"During the early days, our biggest challenge was to determine where the growth capital was going to come from," remembered Miller.

Interestingly enough, until late 1980, we didn't have anyone with an accounting background within the organization. We didn't have anybody with a financial background, and between my wife and I, we did those jobs.

We learned what debentures were. We had to learn all those sorts of things . . . and I kind of converted myself from a biomedical engineer to whatever it was Biomet needed at the time.[2]

Although the bond sale was successful, the founders knew it wouldn't bring in enough, and they had always planned for Biomet to one day be

---

The sale of reconstructive devices in the 1980s would cause a transformation in society that Dane Miller called "dramatic" and "positive."

a public company. So, with a rapidly expanding product portfolio and a widespread network of distributors and salespeople, Biomet took the next step to financing its growth. In 1982, the company laid plans for its initial public offering (IPO), opting to sell stock on the NASDAQ over-the-counter exchange. The offering took place that October; Biomet raised $1.43 million through the sale of 110,000 shares at $13 each.[3]

The IPO was held in conjunction with the sale of 125,000 shares of stock at $10 each to holders of Biomet's debenture bonds.[4] As Ferguson remembered it, most of the bond holders exercised their warrants and purchased stock.

In addition to simply raising needed money, the stock offering had another advantage. By and large, Biomet had grown quickly because of its relationships with independent distributors, so before the time came to offer the company stock for sale, Biomet's founders offered stock options to the distributors to reward them and cement their loyalty. At one point, Dane Miller estimated that the sales force owned as much as 15 percent of the company.[5]

Yet as important as they were, sales reps were only one link in the distribution chain. In the days before managed care and hospital buying groups, the decision to use Biomet's products was usually made by orthopedic surgeons, so it made sense to also offer the debentures to the company's ultimate customers.

"Management felt that getting the debentures into the hands of orthopedic surgeons who were either users or potential users of the company's products would develop a brand loyalty within that community and hopefully establish in the surgeons' minds [the idea] that they were affiliated with a growing, successful enterprise," said Berkley Duck, who helped manage Biomet's first foray into the public securities market. "I think [the founders] had the vision that the company would create a lot of wealth. They also wanted a vehicle so that they could share that wealth with their team members and had an option plan from almost the beginning of the company's history as a public company."[6]

Eight years later, the *Wall Street Journal* would name Biomet the second-most-successful company to go public in the 1980s.[7]

Building Blocks

The money raised from the sale of stocks and converted debentures was put to use quickly. In 1982, the same year it went public, Biomet added 9,000 square feet to its still-new headquarters building. Most of the space was meant for accounting, technical, and marketing personnel.[8] With new offices came new professionals.

"That's when we knew the company was going to make it," Norma Ferguson laughed. "When they fired us."[9]

The founders took their wives out to dinner one night and presented them with plaques. The plaques read, "For understanding, for willingness to take a chance, and for lots of hard work, Biomet really appreciates one of its founders . . . " preceding each woman's name.[10]

"It was really nice. I think they thought it would soften the blow," Norma Ferguson said.[11]

"It was time for us all to leave and do something different," Mary Louise Miller said. "We were all fine with it. We needed to be home more, and we were also starting to do a lot of entertaining in our home."[12]

As the women went into "early retirement," Biomet's management team grew. By the end of the year, the four founders had been joined full-time by Charles Niemier, CFO; John McDaniel, director of product development; James Nicholas,

Charles Niemier, senior vice president of international operations at Biomet, was the company's first auditor. He joined the team in 1980, a challenging time to balance the books.

director of implant manufacturing; Michael G. Hall, vice president of marketing; John A. Smith, director of communications; Garry England, development engineer; and Lee A. Ritchey, production control manager.[13]

Ritchey recalled the headquarters expansions in the early 1980s.

We were pretty frugal in our expenditures, and we did a lot of the finishing work ourselves on Saturdays and Sundays. Dane always kept a pair of coveralls hanging right behind his door. One evening Dane and I were working on the cafeteria. We had the flooring and all the drywall up, and we were setting the kitchen cabinets and sink. It was getting late—we'd probably been at it for over 12 hours. The drill wasn't working very well, so I went down to manufacturing and got a new drill bit, and still you had to lean on it and lean on it to get it to drill a hole properly. I took a closer look at it and [realized] we had it in reverse. I'm thinking, "Here we are, the CEO of the company, and I'm a college graduate. . . ." I said, "Dane, I think it's time to call it an evening." That's one of the things I still chuckle about.

I truly believe that out of a thousand companies in the United States, you would be hard pressed to find one that would have been better to have been with.[14]

Beyond the Numbers

Sales in 1982 jumped some 74 percent, reaching $3.5 million.[15] The implant product group, whose sales jumped 124 percent for the year, produced the lion's share. Two categories, reconstructive and internal fixation devices, accounted for 64 percent of sales.[16] Soft goods accounted for 35 percent of the company's total sales volume. Operating room supplies made up the balance.[17]

Although they were remarkable, the numbers reflected only the surface of what was occurring. Biomet's founders had entered a risky field, but they benefited from several advantages. Due to their depth of experience in orthopedics, they had been able to attract seasoned reps and innovative doctors with ideas for new products. In the

Garry England, senior vice president of Warsaw operations, came to Biomet in 1982. He and founder Dane Miller worked closely with Dr. Tom Mallory to design a femoral component of a hip prosthesis. The product was combined with the work of Dr. William Head in 1986 and introduced as the Mallory-Head Hip Replacement System.

infancy of the modern medical-device business, product innovation often came from outside the companies themselves—through carefully cultivated relationships with physicians. At Biomet, Dr. Tom Mallory—the doctor who once thought it was "crazy" that Dane Miller and his group were trying to break into the orthopedic business—was one of these partners.

Throughout the early 1980s, Mallory worked with Senior Vice President of Warsaw operations Garry England and Dane Miller on a femoral component of a hip prosthesis.

"I wanted to radically change the design of the femoral component from a pipe to a taper," Mallory said. "Miller was very enthusiastic about it, but particularly Garry England, [also] an engineer by training, got excited about it. We created a relationship, and they began to develop this tapered stem. Lo and behold, the relationship was absolutely spectacular."[18]

While this new hip was still in development, the company was celebrating product launches in other areas. This depth of portfolio was entirely consistent with the philosophy of the company's founders: They didn't believe in focusing all of their resources on just one or two "home run" products. Instead, they favored a large selection of solid products in a variety of markets. So while

Mallory and his Biomet team were working on an improved hip implant, the company was preparing to introduce its first blockbuster implant, the AGC (Anatomically Graduated Component) Total Knee System.

Unveiled in 1983, the AGC Total Knee was the first system to offer complete component interchangeability. It consisted of cobalt chromium alloy femoral and tibial components and compression-molded polyethylene tibial components. The knee was innovative for its use of molded polyethylene, something that Miller began working on in graduate school and later insisted be used in the AGC knee.

Dr. Merrill Ritter, the physician who worked most closely with Biomet during the AGC knee development, said the use of compression-molded polyethylene was the key to the AGC knee's 98 percent success rate.

"Dane had a major say-so in utilizing this particular development in polyethylene, and that was foresight because nobody at that time really knew anything about it," Ritter said in 2001. "The knee we put in in 1983 is identical to the knee we put in today. There have been no major changes to the design or the plastic. It's been a great avenue."[19]

John McDaniel, an engineer at Biomet from 1979 to 1986, designed the anatomically graduated component knee in five sizes to fit a spectrum of human bodies.

"The human anatomy varies hugely," McDaniel said in a later interview.

Often implants didn't fit very well. The ligaments don't harmonize with the motion of the knee implant.

The other thing is sometimes you would get a component that would fit one half of the knee, but the mating component for the other half of the knee wouldn't fit the tibia for that particular patient. With the AGC knee, we made all those interchangeable. That was probably one of our first major, broadly marketed products that appealed to a national market.[20]

Although the AGC knee would become one of the most clinically successful total knee systems in the orthopedic industry,[21] its acceptance came slowly. While the AGC system allowed a surgeon to align the patient's ligaments precisely so that the joint worked properly, difficulties arose in getting the ligaments to work with the AGC implant device. This problem delayed the product's widespread acceptance for two years,[22] until the patented AGC Calibrated Distractor debuted in 1985.[23] The distractor correctly balanced and aligned the stabilizing soft tissue—the ligaments and tendons—surrounding the knee.[24]

"It was a fixed-bearing, molded knee," said Tony Fleming, vice president of research and development, "and the molding of polyethylene was critical to its success. It has been implanted now for well over 20 years, and the ones that have been taken out show very little wear. It's sort of the gold standard of Biomet knees."[25]

A Growing Venture

In 1983, Biomet again expanded its headquarters, this time by 12,000 square feet, to boost the facility's total to 44,000 square feet.[26] The company also split its stock twice that year, in March and July.[27] Then in August, Biomet went to the market with its secondary public offering, raising $11.9 million.[28]

Sales would again surge in 1983—to $7.1 million[29]—and the company was ready to act on the next phase of its growth plan. In its first six years, Biomet had derived the majority of its sales from reconstructive devices (at more than 50 percent of total sales) and stainless steel internal fixation devices (at 22 percent of sales).[30] But strong products wouldn't be enough in the long run. The orthopedic industry was booming as the pool of potential implant patients

Biomet's 1983 stock offering announcement, which raised $11.9 million. That money would be used in 1984 to make the company's first acquisition.

steadily swelled. Even into the late 1970s, hip implants had been considered only for senior citizens. By the early 1980s, however, because of better implants and longer-lasting materials, the age threshold was dropping rapidly, meaning the total number of implant surgeries in the United States was rising. Through a fortunate quirk of timing, Biomet was standing on the cusp of this change.

Yet, as with many rapidly organizing, growing industries, success created unstable and dangerous business conditions. Throughout the 1970s and even into the early 1980s, the major pharmaceutical companies saw the opportunity in the booming medical device industry and waded in, buying up any medical device companies they could. Pfizer, for example, purchased Howmedica, while Zimmer was bought by Bristol-Myers. The drug companies assumed they could rapidly scale up the businesses, but this assumption proved wrong, and by the late 1990s, many pharmaceutical companies would divest their device subsidiaries, which would then begin their own wave of consolidation. Some analysts speculated that device companies often suffered from the same supertanker mentality that dominated established pharmaceutical companies.

But in 1984, still fresh from its second offering and boasting annual sales of $10.6 million,[31] Biomet had no way of predicting business trends. It only knew that to survive, it would have to stay ahead of the field.

Fortunately, the founders had anticipated the pressure to grow and, early that year, Biomet made what Miller later called "probably the riskiest business decision in our early days."[32]

David Buys Goliath

On May 18, 1984, Biomet completed its acquisition of Orthopedic Equipment Company (OEC), based in Bourbon, Indiana, with its Canadian subsidiary and OEC Orthopaedic, an English corporation. Founded by a former Zimmer employee, OEC was owned by Diasonics when Biomet bought it. Diasonics was a once high-flying ultrasound imaging company that had run into troubles and was selling its non-core operations.[33]

Although the companies shared product lines, geography, and history, OEC presented significant risk. It was more than twice the size of Biomet, in terms of both revenues and employees, and Wall Street reacted negatively to the news.

"Our stock got pounded," Miller said. "Wall Street wanted to know what a $10 million company was doing buying a $20 million company, and they were sure we were going to get into trouble." Biomet's stock dropped 50 percent.[34]

Wall Street analysts weren't the only naysayers. Three of Biomet's four founders had worked for OEC—Jerry L. Ferguson as director of marketing, Niles Noblitt as director of technical services, and Ray Harroff as product manager. Ferguson and Harroff were lukewarm, at best, to the idea.

"Jerry and Ray thought it was a big mistake," Miller said. "They knew how troubled OEC was, and they didn't have a lot of confidence that we could turn it around. But Niles was real supportive and real confident that OEC could be fixed."[35]

Fixing OEC, however, required Biomet to move quickly.

"Almost instantaneously we had to lay off a handful of people," remembered Miller. "All of them

Biomet's early-1980s board of directors included (standing, from left) Gordon Medlock, Mack Solomon Jr., Jerry Miller, and Kenneth Miller; and (seated, from left) Ray Harroff, Dane Miller, Jerry Ferguson, Niles Noblitt, and Michael Hall.

THE WINGS OF BIOMET

BIOMET'S CUSTOMERS ARE BUSY PEOple. And Biomet is not exactly in a convenient location. This set of circumstances quickly led the company to take its business to the skies.

"Dane is a pilot himself, and he's always appreciated the fact that Warsaw, Indiana, is a tough place to get in and out of," said Tom Allen, vice president of international operations.[1]

The closest commercial airports, in Fort Wayne and South Bend, are an hour-plus drive, and the Warsaw Municipal Airport sits about a half mile from corporate headquarters.[2] Biomet's location is one of the primary reasons the Aviation Department, made up of two Cessna Citation Vs—nine- to ten-passenger aircraft— and one Canadair Challenger, has flourished at Biomet, said Pilot Greg Garber.[3]

"There's a cost of doing business everywhere," Garber said. "In Warsaw, Indiana, it's probably not as high in labor costs and taxes as maybe it would be on the East Coast, but traveling is difficult. That's one of the drawbacks."[4]

The primary use of the department is a marketing program developed in the mid-1980s, the Corporate Tour. Surgeons are picked up at their local airports and flown to Biomet headquarters, where they see products firsthand and speak to the engineers who designed them, as well as the product managers.[5]

The department also moves team members from place to place. Software installed in 2000 tracks what team members' time costs the company when they use another form of transportation, such as flying a commercial airline or driving a car.

"What we have found is that we probably should have been using the airplanes more through the years," Garber said. "It's amazing how easy it becomes to justify. The airplanes are expensive to operate, but having a bunch of employees out driving around all over the country is more expensive oftentimes."[6]

When Biomet leaders embarked on the tours, they quickly discovered how little time surgeons had.

"On the other hand, if you pick them up in a private aircraft, you bring them in, they get business done, and they're back home at a reasonable hour, they'll agree to that," Garber explained. "We'll target a specific region of the country and try to get as many doctors on board as possible to get the most bang for the buck."[7]

Garber's first contact with Dane Miller, however, was not as a team member. Garber was Miller's flight instructor at the Warsaw Municipal Airport. "This fellow walked in and wanted to buy an airplane and needed somebody to teach him how to fly the thing," Garber recalled. "I taught him how to fly in a Cessna 152 that he had purchased. As soon as he got his license, he sold it and bought a Cessna 172 and had that for a number of years. He currently has a Piper Saratoga."[8]

Miller had the right instincts to learn to fly. His father had also been a pilot. But what Miller didn't have was adequate time.

"Although he still has his pilot's license, he has not flown himself for probably four years," Garber said. "He wasn't flying enough to keep current, and he realized that. He decided that until he does dedicate enough of his life to flying—to stay current and stay safe—it just doesn't make sense for him to fly."[9]

The Aviation Department has undergone huge changes over the years. When it began, it was Garber and a six-seat, twin-engine Cessna 340.[10] Upgrades have been made; subsequent aircraft have larger cabins.

"When we're using the airplanes for marketing, I feel the comfort of the surgeon needs to be considered," said Garber.[11]

Opposite: Biomet uses its small fleet of planes to compensate for the out-of-the-way location of its Warsaw, Indiana, headquarters.

were offered jobs back within the next 90 days, but it was extremely difficult to tell people that we were doing something that would change the livelihood of their families. That day became known around Bourbon, Indiana, as Black Wednesday. I don't think anything in my professional career caused me to lose more sleep than that. It was a real tough time."[36]

Laying off team members was not something Miller was accustomed to, but he was intent on turning OEC around—something the staff at OEC appreciated and remembered more than 10 years later.

"It meant a lot to me that those fellows [at Biomet] respected the company they just bought out as well as their own employees," said Delmas Stiles, who had worked in the shipping department at OEC for more than 10 years when it was acquired. "OEC was a great place, but the opportunities [were not] there. They didn't have the growth that Biomet had seen—very few places have seen the growth that Biomet has. So when we came over to Biomet, in a short period of time, you could see that, really, the sky was the limit."[37]

Biomet has taken Jack Wilhite to heights he never expected. A sewing machine mechanic for six years at OEC, Wilhite was moved to the shop floor at Biomet soon after the acquisition. "I learned how to run the mills and lathes. I've got to say it was probably the best move they ever did for me," said Wilhite, a process engineer today.

"I don't have any education higher than high school—it's all been on the job. As Biomet [has grown], there have been tons of opportunities to go different directions," said Wilhite, who has since moved on to computer numerical control machines and robotics. "Just about everything that we've made, I've had some exposure to," he said.[38]

Dane Miller had several meetings with the new personnel in the midst of the acquisition, trying to make everybody feel comfortable with one another, said Bob Border, senior development engineer with Biomet after a 22-year career with OEC. "Dane gave us a pep talk on his goals and ambitions. I can remember, early in the first year, a meeting over in Bourbon. There were probably 30 or 40 people there . . . half of them OEC people. Dane said his goal in five years was to be a $50 million company."[39]

Several people chuckled at the goal. "He actually was able to do that in two years, not five years," Border later remarked. "So I guess the laugh was on everybody else."[40]

When the books finally closed on the acquisition, accountant Charles Niemier remembered it was the first time in Biomet's history that the company "had positive cash flow."

"It was a major day because we were suddenly three times the size," Niemier recalled. "We were a $10 million company, and we bought this $20 million piece of business. It was like David buying Goliath. We never looked back after that."[41]

It didn't take long for OEC employees to realize how hard Biomet would work to seamlessly merge the two companies. Cheryl McIntosh had worked for OEC for eight years before the acquisition and recalled a turning point in her career. About six months after the acquisition, the accounting department was faced with a crisis.

Our vice president was out of town and it was month end. We were trying to get things signed. A week before that I had turned in my resignation. The lady that was in the crisis called the Warsaw office. Well, the only person she could get ahold of was Dane Miller, and he comes in and says, "Okay, ladies. What's the problem?" And he's pushing up his sleeves and saying, "What do I need to do?"

I thought, "This is not going to be someone who is going to say 'OK, you need to do this, this, and this,' and go into some office. He was actually going to help. That is the mentality here. They've had to do it. They've done it to make [Biomet] grow.[42]

McIntosh reconsidered her resignation and is accounting manager today.

Stiles, Trauma Case Department supervisor in 2002, also saw these unique qualities in Biomet's leadership in the early days of the merger. "No matter how much you put in, you always see someone putting in more. You always know that [those in leadership positions] will help you do things that they'll have to roll their sleeves up to do. That is one of the biggest things I've always appreciated about Biomet. I wish everybody had a chance to work here. It's home."[43]

Niles Noblitt made an impression on Wilhite not long after the acquisition. As was the Biomet tradition, supervisors were moved into new, challenging positions about twice a year.

"We were all on the shop floor just trying to figure out who would fit here," Wilhite said. "There were about six or seven possibilities at the time, so I wrote this thing up and posted it on the back of my toolbox. It was kind of a company pool. We each put in a dollar. The next day, Niles comes by."

Wilhite expected a comment about his pool. Perhaps, "What is this about?" or "This is not appropriate." Noblitt surprised all the men when he said, "Can I get in on this?"[44]

The Pieces Come Together

From a strategic point of view, the OEC acquisition could hardly have been a better fit. Although about $2 million of the $20 million business was unprofitable and was quickly disposed of, OEC had a strong line of trauma and fixation products to complement Biomet's total joint implants. Even better, OEC had an established overseas sales network, with a subsidiary in Canada and a large operation in England. OEC Canada (Orthopedic) boasted sales of about $631,000. In Swindon, England, and Bridgend, Wales, OEC Orthopaedic had plants that generated sales of about $7.8 million.[45]

John Deming, a retired Biomet project engineer, called the "mouse-that-swallowed-the-cat" acquisition shrewd despite the early stumbling blocks.

"OEC had a good sales distribution force, and it also had some product lines that Biomet really wasn't into at that time," Deming recalled. "We were into fracture fixation devices at the Warsaw building, but not really to the extent that OEC was, and that's where the big gain comes."[46]

Much of the OEC machinery consisted of World War II pieces. "They still carried the war tag from when [the government] went around and took inventory back in World War II and identified all the machines in the country," said Deming.[47]

By 1985, with the acquisition completed, Biomet made some organizational changes to adjust to its new size and reach. In Canada, product distribution was shifted from OEC's unprofitable subsidiary to Ingram and Bell, a distributor, and Biomet products were added to the pipeline.[48]

Throughout North America, duplicate manufacturing and support activities were combined. All data processing, finance, and accounting activities were consolidated within the Bourbon, Indiana, headquarters. Manufacturing of total-joint products and soft goods was transferred to Warsaw. Production for fixation and most hospital supply products was also consolidated in Bourbon. Jim Nicholas, metals manufacturing manager, helped weave the manufacturing operations of OEC into Biomet.[49]

In the United Kingdom, peripheral warehouse and showroom facilities in London were discontinued and incorporated into facilities in either Swindon, England, or Bridgend, Wales. Marketing, accounting, and administrative functions were concentrated at Bridgend, and the high-tech manufacturing process became focused in Swindon.[50]

As a direct result of the acquisition of the OEC companies, Biomet's 1985 sales more than tripled to $33 million. Additionally, net income climbed from $1.6 million to $3.5 million.[51]

Expanding Market Share

Throughout the mid-1980s, the rise in orthopedic implant surgeries continued unabated, even though most other hospital admissions categories were declining. Hips and knees accounted for 95 percent of the market. Shoulder, ankle, elbow, wrist, and finger and toe prostheses made up the remainder.[52] The increase was fueled by an overall increase in athletic activities across the country and by demographic trends. In 1986 the United States Census Bureau estimated more than 11 percent of the population was over the age of 65, and this segment was expected to grow quickly.[53]

That same year, the company prepared to release its new hip implant. During its development, William Head, an orthopedist, had joined

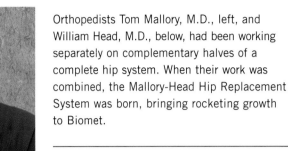

Orthopedists Tom Mallory, M.D., left, and William Head, M.D., below, had been working separately on complementary halves of a complete hip system. When their work was combined, the Mallory-Head Hip Replacement System was born, bringing rocketing growth to Biomet.

the group of Tom Mallory, Garry England, and Dane Miller. The two physicians realized they were working on complementary halves of a complete hip system. When their work was combined, Biomet was ready by 1986 to introduce the Mallory-Head Hip Replacement System to the market.

When it was launched, it was slightly different from the hip replacement systems already on the market, and sales of the product would require a fresh approach. Soon Tom Allen found himself sitting at a table at the American Academy of Orthopaedic Surgeons annual meeting with Drs. Mallory and Head and a hard-charging Biomet salesman named Keith Ross. Allen, who had joined Biomet only a year earlier, was still relatively new to the company and its products. He recalled that his job at this meeting was "don't say anything and take a lot of notes."[54]

It quickly became apparent, however, that the various people involved had different ideas about how the Mallory-Head system should be launched, Allen said.

Tom [Mallory] and Bill [Head] were very concerned. They wanted to get a good scientific project started and put it in a few hands, test it thoroughly, and make everybody come to us and learn how to do it. I could see where this was going. They wanted to launch it, but they didn't want to launch it. So I said, "Look, here's what I think we should do. We need to find a select group of your colleagues who are out there now. You've already trained them to use it because you've been doing it clinically. We've got the approval, and we'll go."[55]

Tom Allen, product manager for the Mallory-Head Hip System, helped doctors develop a presentation to sell the novel system to surgeons. The program was folded into a workshop to educate physicians in the use of Biomet products.

A week later, Allen was named product manager for the Mallory-Head hip. To help sell the novel system to surgeons, Allen helped the doctors develop a presentation called the "Mallory-Head Hip Program." It was folded into a bioskills workshop—an educational seminar funded by Biomet to educate physicians in the use of its products. The first bioskills workshop included a presentation on the best-selling AGC knee, the Mallory-Head hip, and some other Biomet products.

"At our first meeting, I believe it was in Columbus, we had Dr. Dick Scott, who was a good friend of Tom Mallory's, present the AGC knee against the Johnson & Johnson knee [Scott] had developed," Allen said. "We were very confident marketers for those days. We even showed a competitive product at a meeting fully funded by Biomet. But it went well, and most people came out buying the AGC knee, so we had rocketing growth with the Mallory and the AGC."[56]

A Leg Up

By 1986, Biomet needed to expand again to accommodate its rapid growth. In August ground was broken for the third expansion of its Warsaw headquarters. This time, approximately 66,000 square feet of manufacturing and administrative space was to be added, more than doubling the size of the facility.[57] The company also announced expansion plans for Europe, including a move from leased facilities in Swindon, England, to a new, 25,000-square-foot facility.[58]

That year, Biomet's U.K. operation changed its name from OEC Orthopaedic to Biomet. As a result, the registration of the Biomet trademark was extended to 75 countries.[59] By year's end, Biomet products were available in more than 95 countries, with international sales of $14.2 million.[60]

Finally, at the end of the year, Biomet announced that it had retired the SBA loan that funded its early growth. In the 1986 annual report, company executives wrote a note to shareholders to celebrate this milestone.

A final noteworthy corporate event was the early retirement of the Small Business Administration guaranteed loan, initially in the amount of $500,000, made to the company in 1978. . . . The Small Business Administration has served both the company and the country very well. We estimate that approximately $9 million combined of corporate and personal tax revenues related to Biomet have been collected by the Internal Revenue Service as a result of this early funding support. Biomet was obviously a good investment for the United States government.[61]

As SBA Indianapolis District director Robert D. General said, "This is one of the most exciting SBA success stories that I have seen in my 20 years with the agency."[62]

This kind of success was possible because of the respect shared among the founders.

"The four founders respect each other a great deal," Mary Louise Miller said. "They would all four get together for a weekly meeting to discuss things. If they disagreed, it was always behind closed doors. When they leave that meeting, they're a united front. Whether everybody agrees or not, they always present a united front."[63]

A Rising Reconstructive Line

Although the absorption of the OEC companies gave Biomet several valuable product line extensions in trauma, fixation products, and soft goods,

Times-Union   Warsaw, Indiana   Tuesday, August 26, 1986   **5a**

Biomet Groundbreaking — Biomet, the fifth largest manufacturer of surgical implants in the world, broke ground Friday for a 93,000 square foot addition which will more than double the size of the existing structure. Pictured helping with the groundbreaking are from left: Forrest Miner of Farmers State Bank; Jim Nicholas, vice-president of manufacturing at Biomet; Jim Malcolm, architect for new construction; Congressman John Hiler; Robert General of the Small Business Administration; Chuck Niemier, chief financial officer at Biomet; Niles Noblitt, executive vice-president of Biomet; Dane Miller, president of Biomet. — (Photo by Julie Kelsey)

Biomet celebrated two historic events on one day in 1986. Above: It holds the groundbreaking ceremony for a third expansion of its Warsaw, Indiana, headquarters.

Below: Dane Miller burns the $500,000 Small Business Association loan note. The 1978 loan was retired earlier than scheduled.

the reconstructive device category continued to be the fastest-growing and most profitable product offering in the company's entire line.[64]

Sales increased in the reconstructive products category from $17.3 million in 1985 to $26.5 million in 1986, a 53 percent increase.[65] Proving to be especially successful in Europe was the company's line of knee and hip systems, such as the AGC knee and APF hip.[66]

Biomet's 1986 sales rose some 33 percent, from $33 million to $44.1 million. Net income climbed 51 percent.[67] Most of the growth was again concentrated in Biomet's reconstructive products line, which accounted for 60 percent of 1986 sales.[68] "These devices replace deteriorated joints primarily caused by arthritis or trauma," read the 1986 annual report.

A person suffering from a severe arthritic joint experiences an enormous amount of pain, and in many cases, is immobile prior to surgical treatment. A total hip or knee replacement frequently enables a bed-ridden, debilitated individual to move freely and return to normal daily activity within a relatively short period of time. There is a dramatic, positive impact on society by transforming a nearly crippled individual into a productive citizen, thus substantially increasing the person's quality of life.[69]

All Work and No Play . . .

In the days before Biomet's substantial growth, company picnics were a family affair. The field across from Biomet was often transformed into a mini amusement park, and the founders handed out gifts to all the team members' children, Norma Ferguson recalled.

Jerry would take Mark and Michael, our two boys, and then Kim and Stephanie, [the Millers'] girls, out to Kmart. He would tell them to get a shopping cart, and fill it up, and that's where we bought all the company prizes for the bingo games or whatever, and it was almost like Christmas for them. So that was a big treat. It was like, "Maybe you'll win some of these prizes." He always sent them shopping for the children's prizes, and they loved doing that.[70]

Mary Louise Miller recalled the early days of entertaining, namely an annual dinner held at the Millers' home. The house was in the middle of renovations, but they made the best of it.

Biomet team members and their families accumulated many happy memories at picnics. From top: In many years the field in front of the Biomet headquarters was mowed and transformed into a carnival for the annual picnic; not one to stand on the sidelines, President and CEO Dane Miller takes a precarious seat instead; Marie Lowman, accounts payable clerk, rides the bull; before Biomet's exponential growth, children would gather to receive gifts at the annual company picnic.

I made it into a construction party. I had yellow plastic "hard" hats for people when they entered our "construction zone." I took the scaffolding and made it into a bar. We took toy dump trucks and filled them with flowers for the centerpieces of the tables. I even found napkins that said "Caution Zone." It turned out really well, but we weren't fancy.[71]

Twenty years later, Mary Louise would estimate having entertained a thousand people per year, including the annual Fourth of July bash, which involved between 200 and 250 people. Even when entertaining, the founders didn't leave their leadership roles behind.

"We've had employee appreciation days where Dane and the other officers are grilling hamburgers and cooking for the employees and serving," said Regulatory Compliance Specialist Barb Akers. "In my opinion, you just don't see CEOs of a company preparing dinner for their employees, and from what I understand, Dane really likes to cook."[72]

In fact, Biomet officers start cooking at 3 A.M., said Darlene Whaley, vice president of human resources. "We set up a huge tent and have all the team members come out on all three shifts. So we're here at 3 o'clock in the morning, feeding the third-shift team members their lunch. It's just a lot of fun. It gets everybody out of the building. All the officers are out there filling people's cups with more punch or whatever and serving the food."

When Biomet has drawings for company-sponsored trips, Dane Miller has a special technique, Whaley said.

"He likes to torture people," she said. "We crowd up the break room and try to get Dane to talk as loud as he can and do drawings. He'll pull 10 names out of the hat and then put those 10 back in and redraw, with the last one being the winner. So it gets pretty suspenseful at times."[73]

The cover of Biomet's 1988 annual report focused on the company's commitment to providing cost-effective products to enable people to lead productive, pain-free lives.

CHAPTER THREE

STRUGGLING THROUGH EXPANSION

1987–1989

I find it astounding that an upstart company can come into an industry that is so solid and set in its ways and make such an incredible impact in such a short time.

—Dave Montgomery, vice president of sales, 2001

BIOMET'S TENTH ANNIVERSARY, in 1987, was a happy one. The company had posted ten years of surging sales; it had designed and introduced innovative products for a growing market; it had acquired a company twice its size and established itself in Europe; and it had become a public corporation. Although still relatively small, Biomet had attracted the attention of national investors, who were watching the medical industry closely and knew a good thing when they saw it.

That year, Biomet ranked number 89 in *Business Week*'s 100 "Hot Growth Companies" and 16th in *OtC Review*'s "NASDAQ's 100 Fastest Growing Companies." It also earned a place in *Value Line*'s prestigious "Investment Survey" and *Consumer Guide*'s "100 Best Rated Stocks." *Consumer Guide* awarded Biomet a perfect score of 100, indicating that all the brokers following the stock rated the company a "buy."[1]

This praise was earned in an environment of rapid growth through continued product innovation and the development of Biomet's unique culture. In 1987, the company introduced the Bio-Groove Total Hip System, featuring Biomet's latest implant surface technology, which used hydroxyapatite, a naturally occurring mineral that is also an essential ingredient of bone.[2]

The Bio-Groove system had several advantages over its competitors. Machined grooves in the acetabular and femoral components took the place of the porous coating used on competitive implants. These grooves enabled soft tissue and bone to attach to the implant, thus eliminating the need for bone cement.[3] In addition, like Biomet's other successful implants, the Bio-Groove system offered a modular design that allowed surgeons to choose the best size for their patients.[4]

Culturally, it was becoming more and more apparent that Biomet would remain a unique company. This difference—in attitude, dress, and even organization—was immediately apparent to anyone who spent time at the company's Warsaw, Indiana, headquarters. Even ten years after its founding, Biomet still closely resembled the company that had once been run from a converted barn by three engineers and an expert in marketing. For example, team members were expected to take care of anything that needed taking care of. It was a source of great pride among

---

Vice President of Sales Dave Montgomery worked for a competitor for 10 years before joining the Biomet team. He would later call the move a fortunate one.

The culture at Biomet always includes fun.
Above left: John Deming, Martin Bargerhuff, Kim Parcher, Dave Goshert, and John Amber line up for a 1988 Ugly Tie Contest.

Above right: Senior Regulatory Affairs Specialist Lonnie Witham turns into Elvis for special occasions.

Below left: Quality inspectors Kathleen Carper and Kay Heckaman dress for Halloween.

Right: Vice President of Research and Development Tony Fleming enjoys the informal, "hands-on" culture of Biomet.

Biomet team members that the company had no formal organizational chart: If something needed doing, it got done. There was no passing the buck.

Long before the era of dot-com casual, Biomet maintained the informal dress code of its earliest days. According to Tony Fleming, vice president of research and development, who started in 1983 as an engineer, this informality had to do more with the character of the team members than with a plan. "I think one reason we were casual is because we were all hands on," Fleming said.

As engineers, we would get out into the shop frequently. At the end of the day, when I first started . . . we would go out, after the machine operators had gone home, to see what had been made that day. We would just sort of walk around and take a visual inventory or [see] what parts were moved and how far along different products had made it through the manufacturing process.[5]

Buying EBI

At first glance, Biomet's acquisition of Electro-Biology, Inc. (EBI), of Parsippany, New Jersey, seemed out of place. Its main product line was the EBI Bone Healing System, a noninvasive

device that used electromagnetic fields to heal bone fractures.[6] Biomet reasoned, however, that EBI would be a valuable addition to Biomet's overall product mix, bringing a complementary technology that accomplished some of the things Biomet's other offerings did. Although it was based in the United States, EBI had operations in Guaynabo, Puerto Rico, and Reading, England.[7] The company held approximately 60 to 65 percent of the domestic market in electromagnetic bone healing.[8]

Although Biomet and EBI had been in merger discussions for two years, Biomet's initial offer of $6.25 per EBI share, tendered in late September 1987, was unsolicited. EBI had envisioned a joint marketing agreement between the companies, not an outright takeover. By autumn 1987, however, EBI had become ensnared in expensive patent litigation and was feuding with the Food and Drug Administration (FDA), leading Biomet to prefer to buy EBI.

When Biomet's offer of $6.25 hit Wall Street, where EBI's stock had been trading at $4 or $5 per share, it found a ready reception. In early October, alarmed at the prospect of being taken over, EBI announced it was looking for a white knight to stop the acquisition. Hearing its shares were in play, investors flocked to EBI's stock, driving the price up to more than $8. Biomet was unwilling to pay the inflated price and made a decision to unload its stock at the higher price if indeed a white knight did materialize.

Biomet, however, never had a chance. On October 19, 1987—a date later known as Black Monday—about a week before the Biomet offer was set to expire, the New York Stock Exchange plunged an astounding 508 points, or 22.6 percent.

Above: EBI's facility in Parsippany, New Jersey, in 1988. The EBI acquisition, while a challenging one, made Biomet a leader in the electrical stimulation and external fixation markets.

Below: Team members on Hawaiian Shirt Day in the mid–1980s. Seated from left are Marge Gregory, Gloria Castillo Bloch, Pam Canterbury, Sheila Hoover, Naomi Campbell, Kathy Hoover, Deb Cheek, and Barb Blair Akers. Standing from left are Dan Cordill, Scott Charlton, Paula Hoesel, Sam Stutzman, John Amber, Lonnie Witham, Susan Freedle Biggs, Dave Goshert, Vickie Love Adkins, Garry England, Jay Stackhouse, Lyna Moriarty, and Larry Stover.

1988 EBI officers, clockwise from top left: Brian Pethica, Niles Noblitt, John L. Ross, John S. Moore, and James Pastena; Bartolome Gamundi (inset)

The reasons for the precipitous crash were complex, but its effect was clear: in a single day, about $560 billion vanished into thin air and almost every stock on every major exchange lost value. EBI, which had been trading at almost $9, was driven beneath $5.

Biomet, of course, still had an active cash offer of $6.25 per share on the table. Later, Dane Miller would tell a writer from *In Vivo: The Business and Medicine Report* that he heard "that for about a week after Black Monday, ours was the only live cash offer on Wall Street."[9]

EBI's marketing director at the time of the acquisition, James Pastena, recalled the trying times that brought about the purchase.

Right before Biomet bought us, our sales were slowing, and we had had a very nasty lawsuit,

which we had won, but it took practically all our profit that year. EBI was a good buy. We were underpriced. We had good relationships in the marketplace, but I don't think we were as focused managementwise as we needed to be. I think Biomet saw an opportunity to buy us and correct some of these things and turn it around and get it going in the right direction, and that's what they did.

Biomet gave us the ability, the management leadership, that allowed us to focus on our business, which was critical for us. Once we did that, we started to grow. We had good resources with Biomet from a financial standpoint and have done well ever since.

Dane Miller's ability to allow us to do what we need to do has [enabled EBI] to become a nice part of the Biomet corporation.[10]

Less than 10 years later, Pastena would become president of EBI.

Chuck Niemier, Niles Noblitt, and Dane Miller met with EBI investment bankers to wrap up the deal.

"Basically thinking we still have hay in our hair coming from Indiana, this banker starts hammering us," Niemier recalled. "Dane's demands were to remove the outrageous fees that EBI had committed to the investment banking firm and the golden parachutes that EBI's management team had authorized for themselves."[11]

But the tables turned when Dane Miller refused to hike Biomet's offer, Niemier said. Miller stood up, picked up the telephone, pulled out a card, and started dialing a number. When the banker asked Miller what he was doing, Miller replied, "I'm calling that limo service you had pick us up because we're ready to go. I told you what it's going to take to sweeten the deal, and you obviously didn't hear me."[12]

On the way to the airport, Miller, unfazed by the failed meeting, swung through a White Castle for hamburgers with extra onion.

"That story kind of epitomizes everything about Dane and Biomet," said Daniel Hann, senior vice president, secretary, and general counsel.[13]

Biomet stuck with the initial offer and once again began to buy stock from EBI shareholders. By October 28, Biomet had accumulated

72 percent of EBI's outstanding stock, and the acquisition was set to move ahead. On January 4, 1988, Biomet officially acquired EBI, which had boasted sales of $36 million the previous year.[14] The total purchase price was $25.8 million.[15]

Almost immediately after the acquisition was finalized, Biomet was approached by Biolectron of Hackensack, New Jersey, with a $41.5 million offer for EBI. It was a good offer. The deal would bring better than $15 million in profit for Biomet, and Biolectron would benefit from EBI's distribution. Biomet granted an option to Biolectron to buy EBI. In July 1988, however, Biolectron informed Biomet that it had failed to arrange financing and could not complete the deal. EBI, it seemed, would remain a Biomet company.

"Biomet's interest in EBI arose out of a perceived opportunity to achieve long-term growth in consolidated sales and earnings for the company," Miller and Noblitt wrote in the 1988 annual report. "We remain confident that our continued ownership of EBI will accomplish these objectives."[16]

Making It Fit

Achieving those earnings, however, would be easier said than done. Almost from the start,

Biomet learned, EBI would present challenges on several levels.

The first involved EBI's products. While EBI had solid products, they were vastly different from those Biomet was used to dealing with. The EBI Bone Healing System featured a lightweight coil that was worn over a fracture site. It delivered electrical impulses directly to the bone, mimicking the body's natural electrical impulses.[17] Other EBI products included an external fixation system for complicated trauma situations and an implantable spinal fusion stimulator, marking Biomet's entry into

Below left: The EBI Bone Healing System, a noninvasive device that provides therapy for fractures that have not healed on their own, had a success rate of 82 percent. The coil, worn over the fracture site, produces electrical impulses that are delivered to the bone, mimicking the body's natural electrical impulses.

Below right: A component of EBI's SpF Implantable Spinal Fusion Stimulator. In a spinal fusion operation, problem vertebrae are permanently joined, and bony material is introduced in spaces between the affected vertebrae. The Stimulator increases the likelihood of successful fusion by promoting new bone growth.

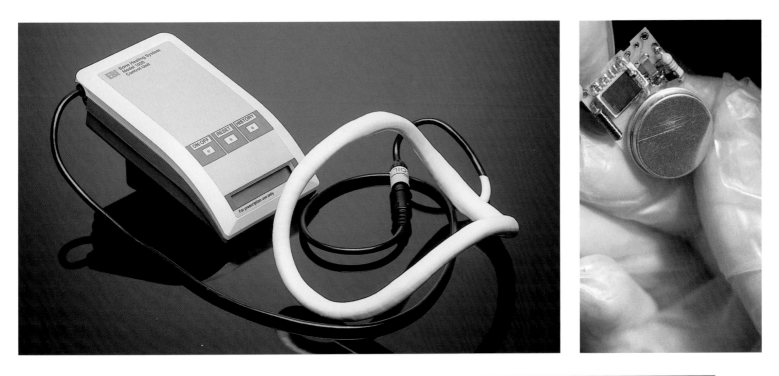

the important spinal market.[18] A spinal fusion is an operation in which certain vertebrae are permanently joined. EBI's SpF Implantable Spinal Fusion Stimulator increased the likelihood of successful fusion.[19]

These products differed from Biomet's other products in terms of customers and sale locations. Moreover, they were paid for by different organizations, including third-party payers such as insurance companies. In contrast, Biomet's implant products were usually paid for directly by hospitals.[20]

"We had never had to worry about whether our (implant) products would get paid for," Miller said. "With EBI, for the first time, we had to figure out who the right payer should be and whether they would, in fact, pay the bills."[21]

These issues might seem like great challenges for a sales force, but Biomet's independent reps were initially enthused about EBI, hoping to find

AN IMPERFECT SCIENCE

NO INNOVATION IS REACHED WITHOUT trial and error. Mistakes are part of any company's history, and although we often perceive it to be, medicine is not a perfect science.

"When it comes to the patient and the patient's well-being, I assign a very high priority to [making] no mistakes at that point," said Dane Miller. "But between here and there, I hope to support an environment where people can make mistakes early in the process so by the time an implant gets into the operating room, it's as perfect as it can be."[1]

At Biomet, money is risked in order to support ideas that come up with new and beneficial products.[2]

"You'll never get a hit if you don't swing," said David Brown, senior development engineer. "The way to make more hits is invariably to take more swings. You're going to fail a certain number of times, and that's all right. There is a real culture to try and to learn from the try. If you haven't had a failure to your name, you're not trying hard enough."[3]

The general consensus at Biomet is that four good decisions out of five are better than two happening very slowly.[4] Failure is part of the discovery process.

"We've done some things that didn't work. We've failed miserably," Dean Golden, director of biomaterials manufacturing, said of products that never made the market. "And we don't beat people up for failure, because we've just found a way that doesn't work."[5]

Jim Haller, vice president of finance, said Biomet is a company that has never dwelled on yesterday. "Right here and now matters, and whatever happened yesterday, you can't change it," he said. "If you're doing what you should be doing right now, the future will take care of itself, so don't worry about it. Move on. You don't have time to sit and worry about your mistakes."[6]

Darlene Whaley, vice president of human resources, said she had "quite a shock" when she came to Biomet from a competitor.[7]

"It was a lot more structured, a lot more political," she said. "At Biomet, it was, 'Just do the work. Don't ask permission. Don't need paperwork filled out. Just do what you think is right and move on.' I can honestly say I made a lot of mistakes in my first few years— but never felt like I was beat up over one of them."[8]

As Biomet has grown over the years, it has had to face the challenges of maintaining control over mistakes. But the company has met those challenges and has fewer problems than its competitors do, according to John Wagoner, director of regulatory compliance.[9] "I think we are doing better at what we have done well," he said. "That doesn't mean we won't have human errors, because, as long as people are involved, [we] will."[10]

a new source of income. Their excitement waned, however, when Biomet announced that the two sales forces would remain separate: EBI salespeople would continue to sell EBI products, and Biomet reps would continue to focus on Biomet products. Miller and Noblitt remembered walking into a meeting with Biomet's top distributors shortly after the acquisition thinking they were "going to need bodyguards."[22]

While Biomet was still working on this issue, a more immediate problem became apparent. Because the acquisition had been technically a hostile takeover, Biomet executives had not been allowed to scrutinize EBI's books beyond what was public information—and they soon discovered the company had trouble. As Miller would note in later interviews, EBI was actually losing money when Biomet bought it. That bad news was compounded by the ongoing litigation and the company's problems with the FDA.[23]

All of this—a hostile takeover, a disgruntled sales force, negative income, problems with the FDA, and impending litigation—combined to sap EBI's morale. Shortly after the acquisition was completed, most of EBI's top executives left the company. But when the sale to Biolectron fell through at the last minute, there was a glaring need to end the chaos and uncertainty at EBI. The next morning, Biomet founder and Board Chairman Niles Noblitt announced he would be moving to New Jersey to run EBI as president.

"In a period of turmoil, there's a lot of tension, and activities can get scattered," Noblitt said. "Our first task was to turn around everyone's attitudes about what they could accomplish. We focused on taking one step at a time."[24]

About a year after Noblitt arrived in New Jersey, EBI was growing again. "Niles rebuilt a management structure and a corporate philosophy within the EBI family and has done a phenomenal job," Miller said.[25]

Nancy Noblitt recalled moving her family to New Jersey. "We'd always been in Indiana, and we just didn't know that much about New Jersey, but we found out that it's very pretty, and there are great people out here," she said, adding that Niles helped turn things around with his skills as a manager and his sincerity as a person. "I'm just very proud of him."[26]

Noblitt's move to New Jersey foreshadowed the shape of things to come for the company's founders. Dane Miller would remain in Warsaw indefinitely, running Biomet, while Noblitt stayed in New Jersey to manage EBI. From then on, Noblitt would perform his duties as Biomet's chairman from New Jersey. Jerry Ferguson would retire in the mid-1980s, only to return in the 1990s, and Ray Harroff would retire permanently in the early 1980s.

Miller and Noblitt were very different managers. Miller was consistently described as an outgoing and "down to earth" manager who was as comfortable giving Congressional testimony as he was walking the factory floor and talking to lathe operators. On the other hand, Noblitt had a passion for the business that was paired with a quiet disposition. John Wagoner, director of regulatory compliance, recalled with amusement a day when Noblitt was mistaken for an intruder.

As Wagoner told the story, an engineer was getting in his car late one evening when he noticed a man walking into the recently completed biomaterials development lab. He followed and asked the stranger, "Can I help you?"

The stranger replied, "No, I just came to look around."

"Did you have an appointment with someone?"

"No," said the stranger. "I just came to look around."

Annoyed, the engineer suggested, "It would be best if you would come back tomorrow. Maybe the person you want to see would be here."

"No. I didn't want to see anyone in particular," the stranger replied.

"You can't just walk in here and look around," the engineer declared. "You need an appointment."

"I work here," was the answer he got. The engineer pointed his finger at the stranger, almost poking his chest. "No, you don't work here, I do. I think it's time for you to leave. Who are you?"

The stranger then said meekly, "I am Niles Noblitt."

Finally the engineer recognized the man in front of him as the man in the annual report photos.

"I thought it was really funny that [the engineer]—a really nice guy—was on the verge of

THE ENTREPRENEUR OF THE YEAR AWARDS

INDIANA BUSINESS SEPTEMBER 1989

ENTREPRENEURS

Dane A. Miller—High Technology

Though we may not like to think of people in medical-related professions as big risk takers, many of them are. In the case of Dr. Dane A. Miller, president and CEO of Warsaw-based Biomet, Inc., risk-taking has paid off for his company, its stockholders and patients needing orthopedic devices, such as knee and hip replacements.

Of course, knees and hips are just a small part of what is done so well by Biomet, and its chief, this year's winner of the High-Technology award. Biomet and its subsidiaries design, manufacture and market electrical bone-growth stimulators, support devices and operating room supplies.

The company was the first in the industry to devise and market a complete joint replacement made of titanium, which is extremely compatible with the body's tissue. "We were laughed at," says Miller.

Biomet grew from four entrepreneurs working out of a Warsaw garage in 1978 to its current 950 employees working in the United States, Puerto Rico, Wales and England. It is now reputed to be the fourth-largest company in its industry. The company's stock was welcomed with open arms when it went public in the early 1980s. Biomet's stock was dubbed the second-hottest initial stock offering in the five years ending in 1987 by *The Wall Street Journal.* ∎

Biomet President and CEO Dane Miller was named 1989 Entrepreneur of the Year in the High Technology category by *Indiana Business* magazine.

removing an officer of the company from the building," Wagoner said. "But as many people know, Niles probably had it coming. You know how some people come to work wearing two different colors of socks? Niles came to work with two different shoes."[27]

Into a New Year

Even without EBI's figures, Biomet posted a solid year in 1987. Although the company's stock had suffered (along with every other U.S. company's), Biomet was in relatively good shape. Sales increased 27 percent, rising from $44.1 million to $55.8 million. Likewise, income jumped close to 55 percent, from $5.2 million to $8 million.[28]

In 1988, once EBI's revenue was included, sales surged nearly 75 percent to $97.6 million. EBI contributed $23.2 million for the seven-month period for which its results were consolidated into the annual total.[29]

Early in 1988, Biomet settled EBI's outstanding $9.8 million patent infringement judgment against American Medical Electronics, of Dallas,

Texas.[30] The complicated settlement awarded Biomet $500,000 in cash; a $1.5 million, seven-year note; American Medical stock; and up to 3 percent of American Medical's revenues over the next seven years from the sale of products that used pulsating electromagnetic field technology, up to a maximum of $2.25 million.[31]

In Warsaw, an expansion was completed that year at a cost of $3.6 million, and construction began on another expansion, which would add 90,000 square feet of office and warehouse space.[32] In England, Biomet opened its new reconstructive-device manufacturing facility in Swindon in January.[33] The 38,000-square-foot facility enabled the company to vacate all of the leased facilities assumed as a result of the OEC merger.[34]

By the end of 1988—a year in which the company was ranked 146th on *Forbes* magazine's list of the "The 200 Best Small Companies in America"—Biomet was the fourth-largest producer of reconstructive devices in the world, behind Zimmer, Howmedica, and DePuy.[35] It held approximately 6 percent of the market.[36] The Biomet board of directors authorized a three-for-two stock split, which occurred on August 22.[37]

The Growing Reconstructive Market

The late 1970s, when Biomet was founded, had seemed like an unlikely time to start an orthopedic company. The FDA had just announced restrictive new regulations for medical devices, and the mature industry was already highly competitive. Yet, paradoxically, it was also the perfect time to start such a company. The aging of America was continuing, as was the development of better technology and new materials that could be implanted into younger patients, meaning Biomet was operating in an environment of rapidly expanding opportunity. The company was positioned perfectly on the crest of a rising wave of potential patients. Between 1984 and 1988, total hip replacement procedures in the United States increased more than 30 percent, and total knee replacement procedures increased more than 75 percent.[38]

Biomet's rapidly increasing sales in the reconstructive device market reflected this trend.

From 1987 to 1988, sales of reconstructive devices increased from $37.5 million to $56.6 million, an increase of some 51 percent.

A year later, hoping for continued growth in this core business, Biomet expanded beyond hips and knees into shoulder and wrist replacement. In 1989, Biomet introduced the Bi-Angular Shoulder System. That year, the shoulder replacement market nationwide was expected to be about $20 million and grow approximately 25 percent per year. For replacement wrists, a market worth about $5 million, Biomet introduced the CFV Wrist Replacement System, designed to enhance both range of motion and joint stability.[39]

By 1989, far from being driven out by larger competitors, Biomet was the only independent, publicly held company with a significant share of the $900 million reconstructive device market.[40]

EBI: Biomet's New Face

Although the reconstructive device market represented the majority of the company's sales—more than 50 percent—its percentage as a share of Biomet's total sales continued to drop. Throughout the 1980s, Biomet had expanded its product offerings, mostly through the acquisitions of EBI and OEC.

As the rocky transition at EBI faded into history, EBI continued to contribute to Biomet's bottom line. The new EBI "product" introduced after the acquisition was a book called *The Efficacy Journal,* which was a compilation of the scientific and clinical papers supporting the use of EBI's main product: the Pulsed ElectroMagnetic Field bone stimulator.

"This was significant in not only addressing the skepticism that existed in the minds of the customers at the time," Noblitt said, "but also reinforced for the EBI team members the soundness of the supporting technology and provided a unifying project during the transition."[41]

In 1989, EBI received FDA approval to expand the SpF-2 line of implantable spinal products, enabling the company to target a new kind of spinal fusion surgery. Approximately 300,000 spinal fusions would be performed annually by the turn of the century, and the move more than doubled the potential market share for EBI's spinal fusion products.[42]

At the 1989 annual American Academy of Orthopaedic Surgeons conference in Las Vegas, EBI released a new addition to its Bone Healing System. This portable device was designed for the treatment of congenital pseudarthrosis, a serious condition afflicting children that often leads to amputation if ignored.

The Decade Ends

As the 1990s drew near, market analysts lavished plenty of praise on Biomet. "No company in this industry has better prospects than Biomet," said analyst Joel Ray of Smith Barney. "We consider the stock an excellent vehicle for long-term appreciation."[43]

Biomet was vastly different from the company it had been a decade before. It had prospered through a tumultuous time that included a deep recession in 1982–83 and witnessed a stock market crash even harsher than the crash of 1929. Yet, for all this upheaval, the 1980s were great years to be an orthopedic company. American industry spent much of the decade with robustly growing sales, and companies like Biomet benefited from continued improvements in its technology and the steady aging of the population.

By the end of the 1980s, Biomet offered products in 70 percent of the product categories in the $1.83 billion domestic orthopedic market—from implants and operating room supplies to electrical stimulation devices and external fixation systems.[44] As its product portfolio had grown, so too had its sales. Throughout the 1980s, Biomet's annual sales grew at an amazing 111 percent compounded rate. In 1989, with a single-year increase of 39 percent, Biomet crossed the $100 million threshold with sales of $135.7 million and split its stock yet again, the second time in as many years. One factor in the sales increase was the inclusion of EBI's sales for a full year. With $43.2 million in annual sales, EBI provided 32 percent of Biomet's total revenue.[45]

As always, Biomet's reconstructive device product line accounted for the majority of the sales—51 percent. Sales in this category, which

Continued expansion of the international market allowed Biomet to completely renovate its offices in Bridgend, Wales.

included the Bi-Metric and Mallory-Head total hip systems, the AGC Total Knee, and the Bio-Modular Total Shoulder, grew some 23 percent to $69.8 million.[46] Biomet's other product lines, including orthopedic supports, operating room supplies, and trauma products, rose 28 percent, from $17.8 million in 1988 to $22.7 million in 1989.

One facet of this growth was Biomet's steady penetration of international markets, which accounted for 28 percent of the company's total revenue. Biomet's strong push overseas began in 1984 with the OEC acquisition, which added manufacturing and distribution in Bridgend, Wales, and Swindon, England. By 1989, sales from the international operation, headquartered in Bridgend, climbed 31 percent to $37.5 million, making international sales the fastest-growing category in the entire company.[47]

In a 1989 interview with *European Trade Report*, Tom Allen, former sales manager for the Mallory-Head Total Hip System and Biomet's new director of international sales, credited the rapid growth in Europe to Biomet's network of "strong and hungry local distributors."[48] These smaller distributors, he noted, were not encumbered by the massive bureaucracy that sometimes saddled multinational medical distribution companies.

At the end of the year, taking Biomet's growth into account and looking with anticipation into the 1990s, Miller and Noblitt wrote shareholders an upbeat letter.

The future of Biomet, if anything like its past, should be very rewarding to the company's shareholders. Structural changes and planning activities at EBI, which were disrupted by the events following its acquisition, are now complete. Many exciting opportunities, both geographically and within various product groups, are open to Biomet. We are optimistic about the future and are confident that our potential is limited only by our imagination.[49]

Above: The Bio-Modular Total Shoulder System for both partial and total shoulder reconstruction debuted in 1988. The system was designed in conjunction with Drs. Russell F. Warren and David M. Dines. Tapered humeral stems, attach to spherical heads, which fit into the polyethylene glenoid (socket) components.

Below: The two photos on the left represent the pre- and post-operative case of a 72-year-old woman with a four-part fracture of the upper humerus. The two photos on the right represent the pre- and postoperative case of a 47-year-old woman who underwent total shoulder revision surgery after developing osteoarthritis of the shoulder socket following treatment of a fractured humerus. Eight months later, both patients experienced a regained range of motion and complete pain relief.

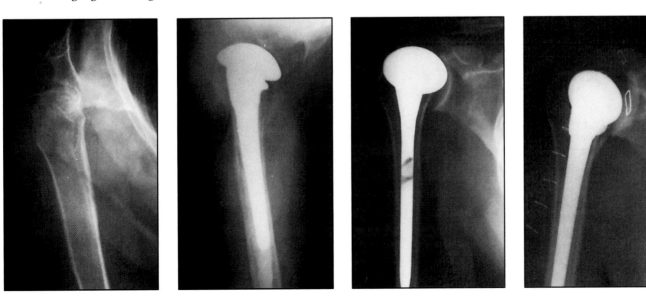

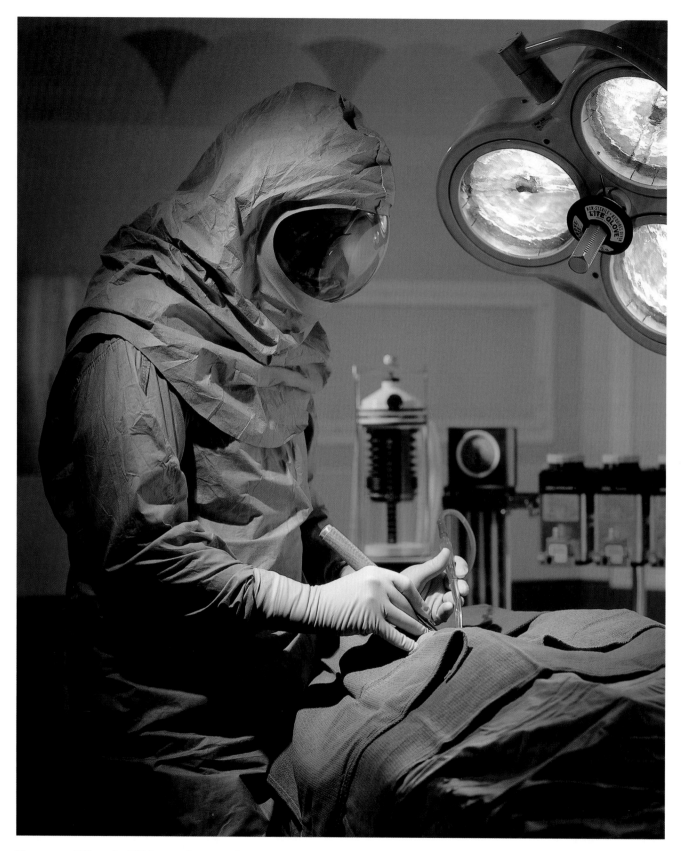

The cover of Biomet's 1990 annual report reflects the company's alliance with orthopedic medical specialists to continue to improve the quality of life for people throughout the world.

CHAPTER FOUR

NO LIMITS

1990 – 1991

The Patient-Matched Implant Department does a lot of stuff basically for no profit. Part of that is humanity and part of it is we just try to cater to our surgeons and our distributors. In turn, they cater to us.

—Terry Martin, director of manufacturing engineering, 2001

THE RUBBER-STAMPED MESSAGE on many copies of Biomet's 1990 annual report pretty much said it all: "Please accept our apology for sending a photocopy. Requests were more numerous than anticipated and depleted our supply of original reports."[1]

Biomet had clearly crossed a threshold. Fresh over the $100 million mark in revenue, the company was steadily gaining prestige in the $1.1 billion market for reconstructive devices, its core market. Even better, this market continued to grow, tracking the U.S. population as it aged and medical science forever pushed the boundaries of health care. In 1990, the number of total hip replacement procedures was estimated to be rising 4 to 6 percent per year; total knee procedures were growing approximately 10 to 12 percent per year; and total shoulder replacement procedures were increasing more than 20 percent per year.[2]

An Aging Population

The aging trend that first rippled through the American consciousness in the 1980s was, by the 1990s, a firm fact of life. According to United States Census Bureau statistics, the general population grew 36 percent between 1960 and 1988, while the 65-and-older category grew by 82 percent and the 85-and-older category leaped 214

percent during the same period.[3] People were living longer, healthier lives, thanks in no small part to medical technology companies like Biomet.

There remained unlimited opportunity for these companies to increase revenue while making a valuable contribution to human health. By the 1990s, most reconstructive joint and fracture procedures were performed to remedy the effects of aging—specifically, forms of arthritis. The term "arthritis" literally means inflammation of a joint, but the word is generally used to describe any condition in which there is cartilage damage. Inflammation occurs in the synovium, the dense, smooth, connective-tissue membrane. The degree of cartilage damage and synovial inflammation varies with the type and stage of arthritis. In later stages, when the cartilage has worn away, most of the pain comes from the pure mechanical friction of raw bones rubbing against each other.[4]

Osteoarthritis, the most common form of arthritis, is a slow, progressive disorder characterized by degeneration of the articular cartilage,

---

Terry Martin opted to leave a larger firm in 1989 to work for Biomet. He was drawn to the company's less structured, "hometown" ambience.

often accompanied by inflammation. It usually affects only one or two major joints, such as in the hips and knees. The cause of hip osteoarthritis is not known. In the majority of cases, it is thought to be simply a result of wear and tear. However, some conditions predispose the hip to osteoarthritis, such as a previous fracture of the joint. Certain growth abnormalities of the hip, such as a shallow socket, also lead to premature arthritis.[5]

In osteoarthritis of the hip, the cartilage cushion is either thinner than normal, leaving bare spots on the bone, or it is completely missing. While bare bone on the head of the femur grinding against the bone of the pelvic socket causes mechanical pain, fragments of cartilage floating in the joint cause inflammation in the joint lining, resulting in a second source of pain. X rays typically reveal the joint space to be narrowed and irregular in outline.[6]

Osteoporosis is a condition characterized by an excessive loss of bone tissue, which results in an increased susceptibility to fractures of the hip, spine, and wrist. Occurring late in life, osteoporosis affects mainly the hands and large weight-bearing joints, such as hips, causing

pain, deformity, and limitation of motion. In 2001, it was thought that one-third to one-half of all postmenopausal women and nearly one-half of all people over the age of 75 were affected by osteoporosis.[7]

Consequently, in the 1990s and beyond, the proliferation of reconstructive hip, knee, and shoulder devices seemed certain as arthritic patients—many bedridden or with severely limited mobility—sought cost-effective treatments.[8]

Expanding EBI

While not all of Biomet's devices are targeted at correcting the deleterious effects of aging, most of them at least have application in that area. A good example is EBI's electrical bone-growth-stimulation products.[9]

At the 1990 American Academy of Orthopaedic Surgeons meeting in New Orleans, Louisiana, EBI launched its SpF-T line of spinal fusion stimulators.[10] Essentially a product upgrade for the company's implantable spinal product line, which was first approved by the FDA in 1989, the SpF-T incorporated a new surface-mounting technology, the use of a flat shape to enhance patient comfort, and an extended battery life.[11] A noninvasive way to monitor the system was also added by incorporating a telemetry device that emitted a signal after implantation.[12]

Once implanted, the SpF-T line of spinal fusion stimulators produced an electric current that passed through attached wires to reach the area where bone growth was to be stimulated. This fully encased electronic device, which was based upon pacemaker technology, began to stimulate bone growth immediately upon implantation and continued for approximately 26 weeks after surgery.[13]

In 1990, EBI sales increased 17 percent, from $43.2 million in 1989 to $50.7 million.[14]

Biomet expanded its reconstructive product line in 1991 with the Quadrant Sparing Acetabular Cup (upper left) and three porous-coated femoral components, including (from left) the Bi-Metric Primary, the Mallory-Head Calcar, and the Integral.

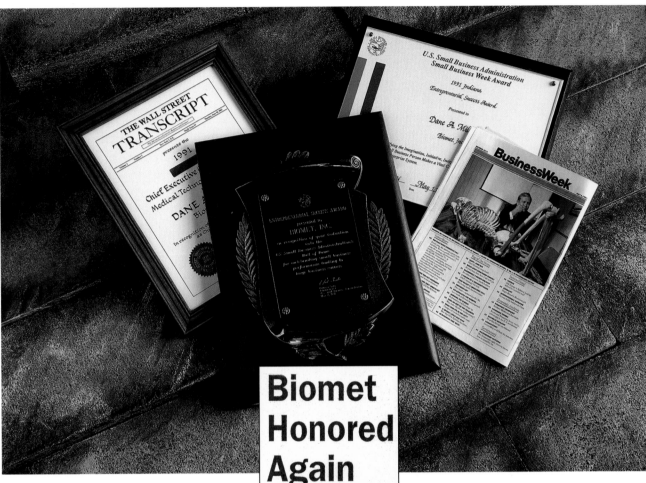

Biomet Honored Again

The Challenge of Growth

Overall, Biomet experienced record financial results in 1990. Sales increased 20 percent to $162.4 million, while net income rose 39 percent to $29.9 million.[15] On December 17, 1990, Biomet declared its sixth stock split, which occurred on January 15, 1991.[16]

Among the honors bestowed on the company in 1990 was inclusion in Standard and Poor's 500 Index of Composite Stocks. For the fifth straight year, Biomet was also included in *Forbes*'s "200 Best Small Companies in America." The firm was ranked first of the 15 companies listed in *Forbes* magazine as "Best of the Best" in earnings-per-share growth, second in sales growth for the prior

NEW YORK (AP) — Biomet Inc. of Warsaw, Ind., a maker of reconstructive joint and bone implants, leads Forbes magazine's "honor roll" of small publicly traded companies with annual sales between $5 million and $350 million.

A survey by Forbes showed that the best little companies in America exploit niche markets with products ranging from medical implants to candy bars.

To qualify for the elite ranking among the Lilliputians of the business world, companies had to post an average return on equity of 17 percent for the past five years and the latest 12 months, Forbes says in its Nov. 11 edition.

Return on equity calculates annual profits as a percentage of a company's net worth.

Additionally, the 15 companies on the honor roll had to show earnings growth of 5 percent over the past year and be among the best small companies cited by Forbes in four of the last five years.

Forbes annually evaluates thousands of small companies, screening out those with declining sales or earnings as well as those with stock prices under $5. Also eliminated are companies with fewer than 1 million shares outstanding or average daily trading volume of under 1,000 shares.

five years, and first in terms of stock appreciation. Lastly, *US News and World Report* ranked Biomet number fifteen in its "US News Stock 100" honor roll.[17]

Above: Biomet received kudos from several publications and business associations in 1990 and 1991, including listings in the S&P 500 Index and in *Forbes*'s "200 Best Small Companies." *Business Week* named Dane Miller the top executive for shareholders' return in relation to executive compensation.

Left: A 1991 news clipping from the Warsaw *Times-Union* highlighting Biomet's honor-roll status. *Forbes* recognized 15 small, publicly traded companies with annual sales between $5 million and $350 million.

100 percent for more than a decade. The founders had "resisted the temptation to act big just because we were getting big," as Miller put it.

"Changes required to support growth will require careful maintenance of the entrepreneurial environment that brought us to where we are today," Miller said in a 1991 interview, stressing the importance of "not getting ourselves caught up in the bureaucratic procedures that tend to slow larger, more mature organizations down. We have been able to achieve that maintenance of an entrepreneurial environment as we've grown from 7 to 10 to 30 and so forth, up to $200 million, and I think if we maintain a careful watch, . . . we can continue to cut a growth rate [such as] we've seen in the past."

Jim Babcock, who joined the company in 1990 from a competitor and later became marketing director of trauma products, noticed the lack of bureaucracy immediately. Like many who moved to Biomet from larger corporations, he was surprised to find a minimalist administration.

Left: Biomet Chairman Niles Noblitt, seated, and CEO Dane Miller in 1991, the company's "year of expansion," which produced net income of nearly $40 million.

Below: Biomet's international officers in 1991, from left: Gordon Howells (Bridgend); David J. Moorse; Robert A. Forster (United Kingdom); Keith W. J. Wright; Mark White; and Norman G. Hibbins (Swindon)

All of this growth, both domestically and internationally, and across the various markets it served, had been accomplished without sacrificing Biomet's basic entrepreneurial operating culture. It's true of all companies—but perhaps even more so in the medical industry—that size breeds a set of challenges all its own. As companies grow, they tend to enmesh themselves in webs of politically motivated bureaucracies. Biomet remained flexible and responsive and had little patience for some of the rituals that envelop larger companies, despite the fact that it had maintained an astonishing growth rate of more than

Biomet Plans To Expand Warsaw Plant

BY DAN SPALDING
Times-Union Staff Writer

Here they grow again.

Biomet, which seemingly matches its record sales with new expansion projects annually, has begun construction on a three-story building at its Warsaw headquarters.

As a result of the expansion and continued strong growth of the company, officials expect to hire another 110 people in the next year, said Greg Sasso, director of corporate development and communications.

"That's based on our growth rate, our sales and what our in-

☐ "We're going through some very rapid growth right now," he said. "I'd say a couple times a year, we're expanding someplace."

Greg Sasso, Director of Corp. Development

ternal support is going to need to accommodate those sales," Sasso said.

The orthopedic manufacturer already employs 750 people in Warsaw and 1,500 people worldwide.

The newest expansion project will encompass an additional 43,000 square feet and will be located just east of the com-

pany's building on U.S. 30. Further east of that site is another project, an 11,000-square-foot facility that is still under construction. That project entails a joint venture with U.S. Surgical.

Ground breaking for the three-story building occurred last month and construction should be complete in about 12

months, Sasso said.

The anticipated 110 added jobs won't be concentrated in any specific area, Sasso said. "It's across the board."

"We're going through some very rapid growth right now," he said. "I'd say a couple times a year, we're expanding someplace."

All of the growth coincides with continued record sales. Biomet recorded a 29 percent increase in sales for the fiscal year that ended May 31.

The company's fastest-growing products are still in the re-

constructive device market, which includes hip, knee and shoulder replacement systems. Sales in that area increased 35 percent last year.

The company also enjoyed a 21 percent increase in sales of its Electro-Biology Inc. products for stimulating bone healing.

For the quarter ending Aug. 31, Biomet had earnings of $11.7 million, up 33 percent from the same quarter in 1990.

In March, Biomet bought Effner Gmbh of Berlin, Germany, whose products include arthroscopy devices.

A 1991 article from the Warsaw *Times-Union* reporting the fifth expansion of Biomet's Warsaw, Indiana, headquarters. The growth coincided with continued record sales.

"When I joined Biomet, I found a company in which you needed a very thick skin," Babcock said. "There was certainly encouragement to succeed, but it was better to try something and fail and try something else than not to try anything at all. There was an oral history here; you did not walk to a bookshelf and pull off a black binder that had all the policies and procedures."[18]

In fact, shortly after he arrived at the company, Babcock remembered attending a meeting of managers. After the meeting, he wrote up a summary of what had happened, including a list of action points, and disseminated the memo to the other team members. In larger, more hide-bound companies, this sort of behavior was expected, even rewarded. At Biomet, Babcock was rewarded by a visit from CEO Dane Miller, who kindly got across the message that "if you wanted to talk to another team member, rather than write a memo, you should probably go talk to the person, and if people were at a meeting and didn't remember the meeting, they probably shouldn't have been there."[19]

Perhaps because of this atmosphere, the company continued to post year-over-year

gains. In 1991, sales surged 29 percent to $209.7 million, and net income increased 32 percent.[20] That year, Biomet stock split again, on December 17. In addition, the company added 43,000 square feet to its Warsaw headquarters and finished a separate, 11,000-square-foot building to house its resorbable material technologies.[21]

EBI's sales increased better than 20 percent to $61.3 million. In the total domestic electrical stimulation market, estimated at some $90 million, EBI held a commanding 65 to 70 percent.[22]

Overseas, Biomet's 1991 sales were $50.9 million—up 39 percent.[23] That year, Biomet entered a joint venture with Amplimedical SpA in Italy to strengthen the sales of its products in the Italian market. The company also gained entry into the precollapse Soviet Union when it received an order for several state-of-the-art orthopedic products, primarily its Bi-Metric Hip and AGC Knee systems.[24]

Again, reconstructive devices were the company's fastest-growing product line. Worldwide sales of these devices increased 35 percent, from $90.6 million in 1990 to $121.9 million in 1991, representing 58 percent of Biomet's total sales.[25]

The company's leading reconstructive devices were the Bi-Metric, Mallory-Head, Universal, and Integral total hip systems; the AGC Total Knee System; and the Bio-Modular Total Shoulder System. Additionally, Biomet

The FINN Knee Replacement System offered both resurfacing and segmental component options in a wide range of sizes to address severe bone loss due to revision or tumor resections.

expanded its product line with the introduction of the CFV Total Wrist, the Total Toe, and the FINN Knee Replacement systems.[26]

The first FINN knee was placed into a 21-year-old pregnant woman, remembered the product's namesake, Dr. Henry Ames Finn, chief of orthopedics and medical director of the University of Chicago Bone and Joint Replacement Center at Weiss Memorial Hospital, an affiliate of the University of Chicago. Without the FINN knee, the woman's leg would have been amputated and she might have lost her baby. Instead, she kept her leg, the baby was born, and the knee lasted more than a decade.[27]

"My relationship with Biomet has been the highlight of my career," Finn said.

I do the most complex surgery related to hip and knee replacement in the world, and people come from all over the world to me. Yet I've never had to go to another company for a device, and I think that says a lot. Most people think business is business when it comes to medical companies. Biomet and the individuals that I have worked with have proven to me that they truly care about the patient.[28]

Recalling an occasion in which Dane Miller scaled a 12-foot fence to get a stock item in an emergency, Finn said, "They go the extra mile for the doctor and the patient. In fact, I have been told that in one's life you will probably meet, at the most, five individuals that will impact your life significantly or that you will have great admiration for. Dane Miller is one of those for me."[29]

Entering the Arthroscopy Arena

Throughout the early 1990s, Biomet continued to make strategic acquisitions, either to bolster its sales and marketing network or to enter completely new but related markets. Miller called Biomet's acquisition approach "strategic opportunism." Acquisitions were usually companies or product lines that were either within the orthopedic industry or adjacent to it. The best opportunities were those that took advantage of Biomet's product development, manufacturing, or distribution capabilities.[30]

Biomet moved quickly on opportunities that were priced right and allowed for cost-effective expansion. "We sort of sit back and wait for opportunities to present themselves," said Miller.[31]

In an eight-month period in 1990 and 1991, Biomet made two such acquisitions that gave it entry into the arthroscopy field. In August 1990, the company purchased Arrow Surgical Technologies, in San Dimas, California, and in March 1991 it bought Effner GmbH, in Berlin, Germany.

According to Daniel Hann, senior vice president, general counsel, and secretary, these acquisitions formed the nucleus of Arthrotek, Biomet's arthroscopy operation. Arthrotek debuted its first products at the 1991 academy meeting.[32]

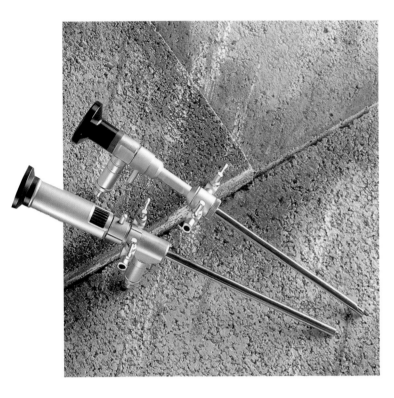

"It's been a nice little success story," Hann said. "It had its fits and starts early on. We had some management challenges, but if you look at the numbers, our product line has grown nicely."[33]

Arthroscopy is a less-invasive surgical approach in which an arthroscope is inserted through a small incision to allow the surgeon direct visualization of the joint. The market had

Left: Biomet entered the arthroscopic arena with the acquisitions of Arrow Surgical in 1990 and Effner in 1991, forming the nucleus of Arthrotek. Arthroscopy is a less-invasive surgical technique using arthroscopes such as these, which are inserted through a small incision to allow direct visualization of the joint using video cameras with fiber optics.

Below: These manual instruments used in arthroscopic procedures are made with a variety of cutting tips, giving surgeons the ability to reach difficult areas.

four basic product categories: power instruments, manual instruments, visualization products, and accessories such as pumps and tubing sets, which allowed the surgeon to irrigate the joint during the procedure.[34] Although it would take a few years for Arthrotek to gain ground, it would become an important contributor to Biomet.

Patient-Matched Implants

Another area that saw explosive growth was the Patient-Matched Implant (PMI) department. In 1991 alone, the sale of PMI products climbed 54 percent. This growth was made possible by the Biomet team's ability to fulfill the needs of both surgeon and patient quickly in what were often difficult and unique orthopedic surgical procedures.

In 1990 the team's responsiveness was enhanced when the company acquired a patent

involving the use of three-dimensional reconstructions in the design and manufacture of Patient-Matched Implants. With this imaging technology—based on CT or MRI data—Biomet was able to assist the surgeon by creating, prior to surgery or the manufacturing of the custom implant, an electronic, three-dimensional model.[35]

The Ultra-Drive Bone Cement Removal System, shown here with disposable tips, reduces the complications and surgical time involved in difficult revision arthroplasty by using ultrasonic technology.

Opposite: Biomet saw a 54 percent increase in the sale of Patient-Matched Implant products in 1991. Shown here is the precision machining of one such product.

A KNIGHT IN SHINING ARMOR

IN A RACE AGAINST TIME, THERE ARE occasions when a knight in shining armor comes to the rescue. Sometimes he arrives in the form of Biomet's Patient-Matched Implant (PMI) department.

Michaela Hennig, of Lakewood, Colorado, witnessed it once herself. At the age of seven, Michaela underwent hip surgery for the removal of a tumor. An expandable femoral implant, made by a Biomet competitor, was put in place. No acetabular (the cup-shaped socket in the hipbone) component was installed in that surgery.

After the operation, Michaela's hip repeatedly became dislocated, causing her great difficulty in walking. Four years later, she was under the care of Douglas Dennis, M.D., of Denver, Colorado, who called Biomet looking for an implant revision to make Michaela's joint functional.

"The problem was [Michaela] had no muscles around her hip joint because they all were removed with the tumor," said John White, director of PMI. "So the surgeon asked us to make a special acetabular cup with a constrained hip joint to [prevent] her hip from dislocating."

Another issue is that a child's acetabulum is extremely small. Dennis also wanted to use Biomet's Metal on Metal, an advanced joint surface technology in hip articulation. "That was a challenge," White said.

But Biomet took on the project. From a CAT scan, the PMI team made a 3-D reconstruction of Michaela's acetabulum and fashioned a custom component that fit exactly in her acetabular socket. Then the team designed a polyethylene constraining ring to use on the acetabulum to prevent dislocation.

"This took longer [to design] than a normal PMI implant," White said. "I think the whole [design] process probably took four months. Dennis did the surgery in June 2001 and said it couldn't have gone better."

Michaela, 11 years old when she received the Biomet implant, has not dislocated her hip since that surgery, White added.

"She's walking around and doing all the things that a little 11-year-old girl should do."

PMI team members often find it difficult not to become emotionally involved in cases like Michaela's.

"There are names and faces associated with these particular projects, and it becomes very personal," White said. "I've got three small children, and I go home every day and think, 'What would I do if this would happen to my child?' I think it puts a little bit more emphasis on what you will accept and what you won't accept and how hard you try to help these people."

Knowing a person is waiting for the implant makes for a stressful experience, White said. "I mean, talk about having some incentive to meet a deadline."

And although the PMI team rarely meets the patient in person, two or three times a year team members actually observe the devices being implanted in the operating room.

"I think it's a double-edged sword," White said. "It's exciting to see these implants go in, and it's rewarding. However, it's also somewhat nervewracking to think that there may not be anything else that can work for this particular patient."[1]

And so it goes. The patient awaits a timely rescue by the cavalry, a faceless team of engineers working feverishly as if the patient-in-distress were a friend or family member.

PMI products range from expandable implants for children to smaller- or larger-than-standard implants.[36] The products also involve nonelective surgeries associated with trauma, primarily motor vehicle, gunshot, and blunt trauma.[37]

"Our engineers work very, very closely with their PMI counterparts," remarked Babcock. "The profiles of the patients are pretty diverse. We had a case last year of a young lady who was 16 years old and riding on the back of a motorcycle on an interstate. She sat up quickly and was blown off the end of the bike and struck by a semi."[38]

In many cases, a patient would fall outside the standard profile and need the implant very quickly. To address this, inventory was often kept at the hospitals or with Biomet distributors.

Although PMI was not a high-volume operation, it was important to the company for a variety of reasons. First, as with many facets of the business, the emotional value of providing relief to the victim of a trauma is a great reward. In addition, PMI has also generated a loyal cadre of surgeons, according to John White, director of PMI.

I think the founders and upper management of this company realize the value of the PMI department, because we basically break even. If we had accountants running the company rather than engineers, PMI would not be here. I don't think you can justify [PMI's] existence with pure profitability. But on the other hand, how do you determine the value of helping a surgeon solve his or her most challenging medical problems? It is impossible to calculate.[39]

The work done in PMI could be a draining experience, White said. "It's just very intense. Everything made at Biomet does a good deed, but in PMI, it's just so much more personal. You know the name, the age, the sex of the person, their diagnosis."[40]

Biomet's custom PMI products are an important component of the company philosophy. The relationship between the physician and Biomet is an intimate one. Biomet is the surgeon advocate, as the surgeon is the patient advocate, explained Bill Kolter, vice president of marketing.[41]

Team members in the PMI department are passionate about their work, and behind every custom product they make is a poignant tale with a happy ending, said Troy Hershberger, director of product development, hips and knees, in late 2001.

They're down there now building an elbow for a young lady. She was walking in a field collecting biology samples and was shot in the hip and the elbow. It destroyed her elbow. The engineer designing the elbow has the newspaper article on the wall so when he walks in in the morning he can see the face of the person he's working on. He just has to justify going home to eat in the evening and going home to bed. He looks at the story and goes, "Maybe I should stick around and get a little more done on this one tonight."[42]

"I can't think of anything better," Hershberger added. "I mean airplanes and automobiles don't hold the [same] fascination for me as working on the human body. You wonder, 'What will those people go on to accomplish because they can walk versus sitting at home or in a wheelchair?' Who knows what it might be? But it really makes you feel good."[43]

Distributor Advisory Panel members in 1991, from left: Tim L. Weis, Martin F. Whalen, George F. Dunican, Susan A. McMahon, Donald S. Marx, and Burton H. Diamond.

Dane Miller met President George H. W. Bush when Biomet was named the Entrepreneurial Success Award winner by the U.S. Small Business Administration in 1991.

Manufacturing Engineer Dan Cordill shared that sense of pride and instilled it in the rest of the team by showing videos of surgeons using the products. "If they see the part going into a real person, it really drives it home," Cordill said.[44]

Biomet was as loyal to its team members as it was to its customers. As a result, some team members walked through the Biomet doors each day with new hips, knees, and other prostheses (Biomet donated its products for surgeries performed on team members).[45]

A Likely Industry Leader

While Biomet received several significant honors during 1991, perhaps the most notable occurred in March, when the U.S. Small Business Administration named the company the SBA 1991 Entrepreneurial Success Award winner. Biomet was honored in a special ceremony held by President George H. W. Bush and the U.S. Congress to recognize the company's phenomenal growth from an eight-person firm—the founders and their wives—to one that employed more than 1,500 people worldwide.[46]

More plaudits followed. In March, the Puerto Rico Products Association awarded EBI the Quality in Excellence Award for its implantable, bone-healing product line. In April the United

Shareholders Association ranked Biomet ninth in its listing of the top 1,000 corporations in the United States and sixth in the area of Best Economic Performers. In May, *Business Week* declared CEO Dane Miller the top executive in the country for shareholders' return in relation to executive compensation. The magazine also named Biomet the top company in the nation for return on equity in relation to executive compensation.[47]

For the second consecutive year, Biomet was named a finalist in the Welsh Export Awards, sponsored by the Bank of Wales.[48] Finally, *North American International Business Magazine* recognized Biomet as one of the fastest-growing companies in international trade.[49]

Market analysts continued to review Biomet favorably. Nationally syndicated financial columnist Malcolm Berko raved about the company in a 1991 column.

The company has a squeaky clean balance sheet, no debt, and a highly skilled, motivated work force. Their sales reps are so good that they are often in the operating room assisting surgeons with implant procedures. Because this company has a highly skilled R&D staff, as well as excellent product quality and design, Biomet is held in high esteem by orthopedic surgeons throughout the country. And Biomet's future is held in similar esteem by analysts, because earnings are comfortably projected to grow at a 30-percent rate through the 1990s.

EBI's manufacturing facility in Puerto Rico. In 1991, the Puerto Rico Products Association awarded EBI the Quality in Excellence Award for its bone-healing product line.

An ad for Arthrotek's 1993 Caspari Suture Punch, shown with the Harpoon Suture Anchor. Prior to the development of these products, the reattachment of soft tissue to bone was a complex and time-consuming procedure.

CHAPTER FIVE

CORPORATE CULTURE

1992–1993

Dane is a very family-oriented person and Biomet is like a family.
Everybody is treated equally. Everybody is important.

—Mary Louise Miller, 2002

BIOMET WAS FOUNDED UPON THE idea that an aggressive, nimble company could respond to the needs of its customers—and the marketplace in general—in a more efficient way than a bureaucratically organized business could. This idea has permeated Biomet's operating culture from its earliest days, and most Biomet team members credit it as a major element in the company's success.

Like many successful concepts, the Biomet cultural mold is not difficult to understand—it is only difficult to mimic. From the beginning, Biomet team members at all levels were empowered to make critical decisions to expedite the flow of new and improved products into the market.[1]

"We try to point our people in the right direction, line them up with the right projects, and then get out of their way," said Troy Hershberger, director of product development, hips and knees.[2]

Dane Miller said Biomet's philosophy not only keeps staff happy, it benefits the company. "Companies that fail to properly motivate and support their most important asset—people—eventually fail or lose their competitive edge in the marketplace," he said.[3]

The founders realized from the beginning that one key to building a responsive and competitive organization would be the creation of a work environment in which individuals would not feel stifled by bureaucracy. They wanted an environment that encouraged team members to accept new challenges. They wanted to streamline the decision-making process.[4]

"We didn't want to end up with a political atmosphere that drove people away from the company," said founder Jerry Ferguson. "The atmosphere needs to be such that people can freely express their ideas, go about their business, and concern themselves with the growth of the company, new ideas, and new products."[5]

No Ties, Please

At Biomet, even 14 years after its founding, there are no memos, no closed doors, no assigned parking spaces, no suits or ties, and turnover is low. The people who work at Biomet are "team members," not employees. Many consider the casual atmosphere of blue jeans and shorts to be part of why people come to work at Biomet, said Steve Stewart, director of sales administration.[6]

Arthrotek's products, such as this arthroscope, are designed for use primarily in knee and shoulder reconstruction surgeries.

"I've seen Dane cut ties off of people at meetings," Stewart recalled. "We've all come to the conclusion that there's no correlation between a tie and doing good business."[7]

Regardless of job level, every team member is given stock options after two years at Biomet— everyone, that is, except CEO Miller and Chairman Noblitt, neither of whom has ever taken a stock option.

Biomet's hourly team members are treated with the same respect that salaried team members receive, said Don Boggs, retired director of manufacturing. The general philosophy is "You can buy a machine, but you can't buy the loyalty of the people," he said.[8]

Above: Dane Miller asks the advice of a monkey during the filming of a spoof for a national sales meeting.

Below: Linda Tyler and David Fulton exchange vows in the break room of the soft goods department, enabling Linda's friends and coworkers to attend. Dane Miller gave the bride away.

"It's a different style of management," agreed Greg Sasso, vice president of corporate development and communications. "Dane and Niles really believe in giving stock options to the entire Biomet team and giving back to the shareholders. All team members have benefited immensely through Biomet's 401(k) plan, which matches $.75 on each dollar in Biomet stock; the Employee Stock Bonus plan, in which the company contributes 3 percent of each team member's salary in Biomet stock; and, of course, the stock option programs."[9]

That steadfast loyalty is also displayed to team members by promoting from within, said Sam Stutzman, director of manufacturing. "On the shop floor, we have 17 supervisors, and every one of those people came from within the ranks of Biomet. All these folks worked their way up from the shop floor and got into management and supervision."[10]

There may be no better example than that of Dean Golden, who took a long, winding road before becoming director of biomaterials manufacturing.

"I interviewed with Dane Miller for a janitor's job as a kid still in high school," Golden said of his 1980 start at Biomet. "I used to take out trash, touch up polishing, and run errands."[11]

Golden moved into assembly and then inspection before going into engineering around 1986. From there he worked in the Patient-Matched Implant department and the legal department and eventually was promoted from manager to director of biomaterials manufacturing.[12]

Many other Biomet team members came from outside service providers, such as Senior Vice President of Finance and Treasurer Greg Hartman, who recalled his first thoughts on the culture at Biomet.

I noticed the difference in culture at Biomet right away. It's a company that recognizes people for their abilities, and when they do the job and get it done, Biomet promotes them, gives them bonuses. Many companies have more of a good ol' boy culture, where if you are there for X number of years or if you have a college degree, it means that you are a better manager than somebody who has worked for 10 years and learned how to do stuff in the school of hard knocks.[13]

Mark Vandewalle, director of engineering services, came to Biomet from a local competitor, where a layered, departmentalized atmosphere created obstacles.

"I was pretty fed up," he said. "It was mind-boggling how difficult it was to get simple things done. It leads to a high level of frustration, and that is common to a lot of people who came to Biomet. They left other companies because of that frustration."[14]

Vice President of Manufacturing Rich Borror—a nonconformist who wears a tie every day—said that many gravitated to Biomet because they had a hard time fitting in elsewhere.

I always—very lovingly—refer to Biomet as the equivalent of the "Island of Misfit Toys." And I include myself in that. For whatever reason, you just didn't fit into what you'd call a normal kind of company. So you find this Biomet thing where Dane and Niles, especially, will tolerate a lot of individual behavior and differences of opinion—things that wouldn't happen in a lot of other businesses.

When you work with guys like Dane and Niles—good people, fair people—[you] like working here and [you] stick around. You can have a genuine disagreement with [them], and it's nothing personal. And that means a lot.[15]

Teamwork

Industry analysts universally cited camaraderie as a key force behind the company's vigorous growth.

"It's a very hands-on management," said Larry Neibor, an analyst with Robert W. Baird & Company. "Top managers are constantly out on the shop floor. They don't sit in a separate headquarters building in some sort of ivory tower concocting plans."[16]

Biomet team members and salespeople routinely interacted on a global basis by discussing and implementing new product ideas, opportunities, and distribution strategies. Team members from engineering, marketing, production, planning, and manufacturing worked in close proximity on common products, forming integrated work teams.[17]

These work teams streamlined the flow of information among development, marketing,

Left: Treasurer and Senior Vice President of Finance Greg Hartman says Biomet recognizes and values team members for their abilities.

Right: Vice President of Manufacturing Rich Borror affectionately refers to Biomet as the equivalent of the "Island of Misfit Toys."

and design team members. As a result, the lines between formal marketing and engineering departments blurred and functional work groups took their place.[18]

To support these teams, computer-controlled-design groups and manufacturing groups were clustered into cells that manufactured similar products, such as hips and knees. The close proximity of people from the various disciplines and machines allowed Biomet team members to make the gradual, incremental improvements that result in better products.

"We at Biomet are very adamant about process improvement," said Dan Cordill, manufacturing engineer, hips. "The idea behind having a group of people work on the same type of parts is that they become the experts. So when we look at our production, we don't just say, 'Let's buy another lathe like the six we already have.' We try to look for a better way to do it, a better way being a higher quality way, a more economical way."[19]

The company's 1992 sales results were a testament to this successful operating philosophy of teamwork, incremental improvement, and personal responsibility. For the 14th consecutive year, Biomet grew in both sales and net income. Sales grew 31 percent to $274.9 million, while net income similarly surged some 31 percent, to $51.8 million. Reconstructive devices, which increased 33 percent to approximately $162.3 million, continued to lead the company's sales growth.[20]

As for the growth in value of Biomet's stock, a shareholder who purchased 1,000 shares of the company for $13,000 in its 1982 initial public offering would have held 36,000 shares worth approximately $693,000 by July 1992.[21]

Product Innovation

The company's research and development efforts resulted in the rollout of several new products at the 1992 American Academy of Orthopaedic Surgeons conference in Washington, D.C.[22]

Among them were the Mallory-Head Modular Hip System (an extension of the Mallory-Head Total Hip System) and the Impact System. These modular hip systems addressed a niche portion of the hip market by allowing surgeons to combine different sizes of proximal and distal femoral components during a hip replacement procedure, thereby achieving an optimum fit for their patients.[23]

Dr. William Head, who had been a part of the hip design team since the 1980s, spoke highly of his experience working with Biomet.

They've been very refreshing and easy to work with in that you don't get bogged down in a lot of bureaucracy. You find out a yes or a no very quickly, and it's easy. They're aggressive and pleasant to work with. Dane is a hands-on fellow. He's a visionary. He seems to have a knack of knowing the right thing to do, the right designs, and also he has a knack of picking the right

LENDING A HAND

IN 1993, BIOMET ESTABLISHED ITS Friends in Need program, a venture having less to do with profit than with patient welfare. While the Biomet team had been long recognized as a company committed to improving the quality of life for individuals, some people did not have the resources or opportunity to benefit from many of the advances that had taken place in the medical device field. Through the company's sales force and its close working relationship with both hospitals and surgeons, the Friends program identified and served patients who needed joint replacements or electrical stimulation therapy and who lacked financial resources.[1]

Imagine life in a country where medical care was not widely available. And when you did find it, it was often not very good. When you and your family were healthy, making enough money to meet your basic needs would be difficult enough. But what would you do if you were not well and could no longer work? What would you do if you discovered there was an operation available that would help you immensely, but you had no way to pay for it?

Livia Bob (pronounced with a long *o*), a resident of Romania, found herself in exactly that situation. So she wrote to every family member she could think of—even those whom she had never met before. Laura Boyd, who lives in Farmersville, Ohio, was one of those family members.

In September 1996, after learning Bob needed replacement surgery for both hips, Boyd wrote a letter to the Biomet International department. She knew about Biomet from reading the company's annual report, obtained earlier by her investment club.

The letter asked the company to sell two total hip replacements to Bob at a discounted price. It was forwarded to Biomet Contract Manager Deb Nielsen. Nielsen called Boyd to explain that far more is involved in a total hip procedure than the implants and then explained Biomet's Friends in Need program. Through the program, Biomet donates products to people with special needs, and, when possible, the company assists in obtaining donations from others in the medical community, Nielsen explained.

Nielsen then asked if the patient could arrange travel to the United States. She

people to surround him. The integrity and the character of the people at Biomet are absolutely impeccable. I'm very proud to have associations with them.[24]

That same year, Biomet introduced the AARS Unicondylar Knee System, which was designed for younger osteoarthritic patients who did not require a total knee replacement. The device allowed for later conversion to a total knee replacement if one were necessary.[25]

While some competitors would consider the product a sacrifice of higher sales, since it replaced only part of the knee, Biomet was looking out for the interests of the patient, said Kevin Stone, director of product development.[26]

Arthrotek, the company's growing arthroscopy subsidiary, unveiled the IES 1000 System as the first truly integrated system for minimally invasive surgery in the orthopedic marketplace. Housed in a prewired console unit—thereby eliminating the time-consuming setup by the operating room staff—the camera, light source, shaver, pump, printer, and VCR system were combined into a single device operated by one remote control.[27]

EBI introduced a full line of FLX-Specialty Flexible Treatment devices—flex coils to address shoulder, foot, ankle, and other fixation applications. These products helped assure the surgeon of a custom fit.[28]

As a result of these product innovations and the rising acceptance of electrical stimulation

also called Biomet sales associate Jeff Cisney for help.

Cisney went into action and secured donations of hospital facilities and patient care from Saint Joseph Medical Center in Fort Wayne, Indiana, for the first hip surgery. Lutheran Hospital, also located in Fort Wayne, agreed to donate the same for the second hip procedure. Dr. David Pope agreed to perform both surgeries and provide follow-up care at no charge. Miami Valley Hospital, based in Dayton, Ohio, volunteered to help with the recovery by donating physical therapy services. Biomet would supply the necessary hip replacement devices.

Boyd and other family members diligently contacted government officials for help in completing the necessary paperwork for Bob's trip to the United States. In February 1997, she was cleared to leave Romania.

Upon arrival in the United States, the patient was mainly wheelchair bound. She also suffered from high blood pressure, and her left leg was shorter than the right due to a poorly executed previous hip replacement in Romania.

Bob's right primary hip replacement was carried out first. A Mallory-Head Porous Femoral Stem, Index shell, ArCom liner, and ceramic head were used. During the second surgery, performed a few months later, only the acetabulum was revised. A Ranawat-Burstein Limited Hole Cup and ArCom liner were employed in the revision surgery. In the process, Bob's leg length was also corrected.

On July 11, Bob, Boyd, and other family members joined Cisney and Nielsen for a tour of Biomet's Warsaw, Indiana, headquarters. The family wanted to express its gratitude to the company and everyone else involved in Bob's recovery.

In August Bob returned home to Romania and to her work as a biology instructor. She was pain free and able to walk quite well with the limited use of a cane.[2]

therapy among orthopedic and neurological surgeons, EBI sales in 1992 grew 20 percent to $73.5 million. With the electrical stimulation market in the United States estimated then to be $103 million, EBI maintained its better-than-two-thirds share of the market.[29]

Lorenz Surgical

On April 23, 1992, Biomet announced it had reached an agreement to acquire Walter Lorenz Surgical in a $19 million stock swap.[30] Founded by Walter Lorenz in 1966, Lorenz Surgical, based in Jacksonville, Florida, was a leading marketer of a complete range of oral-maxillofacial-craniofacial products, sold principally to oral surgeons.[31]

Walter Lorenz was one of the best-known names in his industry. He was born in West Germany and attended Sieburg College, where he served an apprenticeship in surgical instrument shops. In 1958, at the age of 28, he moved to the United States to work in his uncle's dental instrument firm in Westport, Connecticut. Lorenz eventually started his own business, which he ran for ten years before moving to Jacksonville in 1976.[32] By the early 1990s, with his health failing, Lorenz was ready to sell his business—but would sell it only to someone he trusted.

Buying such a well-respected name from a personal friend was something Dane Miller, who negotiated the deal, took very seriously. "We will strive to further Walter's commitment to

Left top: Daniel Hann, senior vice president, general counsel, and secretary for Biomet, was a member of the board of directors in 1993, when the company was authorized to buy back up to $25 million of its issued and outstanding common shares.

Left bottom: Senior Vice President Joel Pratt stands firmly behind the company's manufacturing team, which performed impressively during a critical time in the Lorenz acquisition.

the oral-maxillofacial profession by engaging in research and development programs that will produce new products and techniques for the oral-maxillofacial surgeon," Miller said. "We thank Walter for laying this important foundation."[33]

In fact, it was Miller's relationship with Lorenz that made the acquisition possible. "Lorenz was really an opinion leader in his field," said Daniel Hann, senior vice president and general counsel. "The Lorenz name means something because of him. Dane was very critical to that deal because he had a very good personal relationship with Walter."[34]

The acquisition, however, would not be completely smooth. After it was final and Biomet was preparing to take control of the company, several key executives left Lorenz and launched a competing business. Worst of all, they were working with the same German manufacturer that supplied Lorenz Surgical's product line. Things became critical when the German manufacturer tried to freeze the supply of product to Lorenz.

Jerry Ferguson, one of Biomet's founders, quickly took control of the situation. Ferguson had left Biomet in 1984, only to return in late 1993. He remembered the challenges at the new acquisition.

As it turned out, these guys had been planning their own deal for months. They had agreed with the German manufacturer to leave Lorenz and join a new business. So, in December, we were told that as of January, we would have no more product. Lorenz was doing about $12 [million] to $15 million, so this was scramble time.

I think a lot of people would have said, "Hey, it's time to wrap it up. It's more than we can handle." You're talking about trying to replace thousands of identities—small screws, plates, you name it. That probably would have been a good plan with anybody but Dane. I've always said if you look in the dictionary after the word "tenacity," you should see a picture of Dane Miller.[35]

Plans to dry up Biomet's inventory and leave a sales force with nothing to deliver did not pan out. When the German supplier, in conjunction with the former Lorenz executives, offered to buy Lorenz from Biomet, the proposal was turned down. Biomet quickly moved to show the sales force that it had the manufacturing capability to make Lorenz's product line, remembered Joel Pratt, senior vice president of Biomet.

We flew the entire sales force into Warsaw, and we knew that in order to succeed, we had to have that sales force. So we had to give them some sort of assurance that we could continue to supply product. We asked them to design a plate—something that they didn't currently have, that maybe a competitor had—that would help them sell more product. We asked them to do that at 11:30 in the morning.

When we broke for lunch, I took that information to our manufacturing team, and they programmed a machined part. When we returned from lunch at 1 o'clock, I showed the group the part. They were just dumbfounded. They couldn't fathom how in the world we were able to do that in a two-hour time period.[36]

Sadly, Walter Lorenz did not live to see the full synergies of the merger realized. He died at his Florida home on August 15, 1993, at the age of 62.[37]

Faith in the Future

In May 1992, *Business Week* magazine ranked Biomet number 316 in its "Top 1,000" companies, gauged by stock market value. Also in May, for the second consecutive year, *Business Week* ranked CEO Miller the top executive in terms of return to shareholders relative to compensation.[38]

On January 28, 1993, while construction of the company's Warsaw expansion was being completed, a time capsule was placed in the base of the center stairway of the 65,000-square-foot addition. Marked by a brass plate, and not to be opened until 2018, the capsule included a list of

In 1992, for the second consecutive year, *Business Week* named Biomet President and CEO Dane Miller the top executive in terms of return to shareholders relative to compensation.

As Biomet grew, so did its board of directors. Attorney Marilyn Quayle, wife of former Vice President Dan Quayle, joined the board in 1993.

Biomet's team members, a product list and price sheet, scrapbooks and photo albums, Biomet's first checkbook, a video about the corporation, and several videos about joint-replacement technology.[39]

Despite a modest retraction in Biomet's growth rate in 1993, the company once again reported record financial results. Sales increased 22 percent to $335.4 million, while net income increased 23 percent to $63.9 million. The increase was due to growth in reconstructive devices and the inclusion of sales by Lorenz Surgical.[40] Separately, EBI posted a 12 percent rise in sales, from $73.5 million in 1992 to $82.1 million in 1993.[41] Biomet's international sales increased 11 percent in 1993—from $70.6 million in 1992 to $78.3 million.

By any measure, Biomet had prospered greatly over the years. In 1988, for example, the firm had six locations worldwide; by 1993, it had 12. In 1988, Biomet had 565 team members; by 1993, it employed more than 1,700 worldwide.[42] Impressively, 1993 represented Biomet's 15th consecutive year of increases in both revenues and net income. Over the preceding decade, the company's sales grew at a 47 percent compounded rate, while net income climbed at a 57 percent compounded rate.[43]

As the company grew, so too did its board of directors. On September 27, 1993, Marilyn Tucker Quayle, an attorney in private practice in Indianapolis, Indiana, and the wife of former Vice President Dan Quayle, joined the Biomet

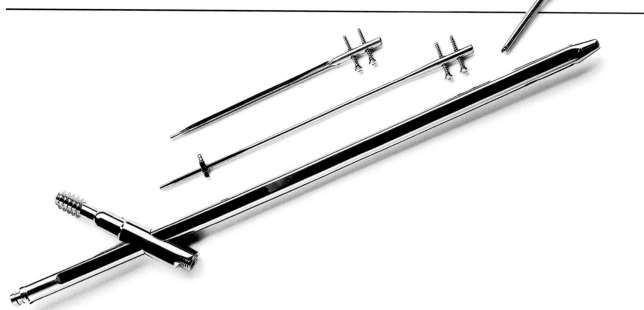

board. Other members included Niles Noblitt, chairman of the board; Dane Miller, president and CEO of the company; Jerry Ferguson, special projects advisor of the company; Daniel Hann, vice president, general counsel, and secretary of the company; Ray Harroff; Thomas Kearns Jr.; Jerry Miller; Kenneth Miller; Charles Niemier, senior vice president of international operations; James Norris; and L. Gene Tanner.[44]

Biomet Reorganizes

Although Biomet had managed to avoid the worst pitfalls of rapid growth, by the early 1990s the company needed to confront the consequences of its expansion. As a global operation active in many different markets, Biomet was due for reorganization, its executives decided. Operations at Warsaw were separated into two units: Biomet Reconstructive Products and Biomet Medical Products.

Biomet Medical was responsible for soft goods, surgical products, fixation products, general instruments, arthroscopy products, hand

Above: The Vector Intertrochanteric Nail was introduced in 1992. It was designed to provide temporary stabilization of fractured bones while they heal.

Below: Biomet founders have created a unique work environment in which team members are not stifled by bureaucracy and unnecessary layers of management. From left are Quality Engineer Clark Rutledge, Soft Goods Production Planner Sherry Wilson, and Manufacturing Supervisor Craig Charlton in 1992.

products, and foot and ankle products, such as the Total Toe System.[45] Biomet Reconstructive Products was responsible for the company's signature reconstructive lines.

It was thought that Biomet Medical would benefit from its own development, marketing, and distribution channels. Company executives worried that the sales and development operations had been overly focused on reconstructive devices under the old organization.[46]

The Maxim Total Knee

The corporate reorganization coincided with the 1993 release of a new, gold-standard knee replacement. Called the Maxim Total Knee, it was the third total knee replacement system offered by the company, after the Total Cruciate Condylar knee and the popular Anatomic Graduated Component knee. The Maxim offered orthopedic surgeons a broad, versatile array of instruments and implants to address a wide range of total knee procedures, ranging from primary knee replacements to complex revision surgery. The system proved to be the most successful new product introduction in the history of Biomet.[47]

Troy Hershberger, director of product development, hips and knees, recalled working on the Maxim Knee.

I hired into the knee group with Steve Herrington—he and I were partners back at Zimmer. The funny thing was neither Steve nor I had ever designed a knee system before, but nevertheless, in Biomet tradition, we were given responsibility way beyond our capability, and off we went. That product ended up becoming the Maxim Knee System, which was our biggest product launch for Biomet, and it soon became the biggest-selling product line in our history.

All the resources possible were devoted to this one project. We really went out on a limb with the resources we put toward it, and it paid off in spades with sales that took our company to a new level of growth.[48]

The Maxim Total Knee System was developed, approved, and released to the market less than two years after Biomet's initial meetings with the developers—Dr. Robert Booth, of Philadelphia, Pennsylvania; Dr. Adolph Lombardi, of Columbus, Ohio; and Dr. Bradley Vaughn, of Raleigh, North Carolina.[49]

The Maxim Knee had abundant advantages. Its state-of-the-art metallurgy included cobalt chromium and titanium. The knee system had complete femoral and tibial augmentations to substitute for bone loss, and anatomic right and left femoral components with a deep patellar groove. Finally, it comprised a large variety of fixation stems to secure the femur and tibia to varying bone quality.[50]

After approaching several companies with their ideas for the Maxim knee, the developers decided Biomet was clearly the most responsive, Dr. Lombardi said.

"They wanted to take our ideas and bring them to marketplace quickly," he recalled. "They recog-

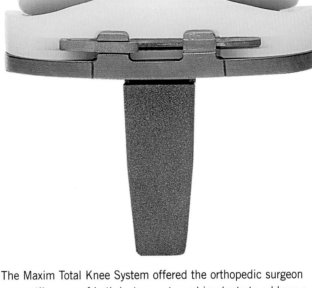

The Maxim Total Knee System offered the orthopedic surgeon a versatile array of both instruments and implants to address a wide range of procedures, from primary knee replacements to complex revision surgeries.

nized the concepts were good and the need was there, and that began a long and very fruitful relationship for us."[51]

While the Maxim Total Knee System was being introduced, Biomet's other total knee system, the AGC knee, continued to win honors. The results of the Swedish Knee Study revealed that the company's AGC Knee had the lowest revision rate—determined by the number of implants that needed replacement due to wear, loosening, or trauma—of any knee system in the study.[52]

The Harpoon Suture Anchor

Another significant product was introduced in 1993 when Arthrotek received FDA clearance to market and sell the Harpoon Suture Anchor. The harpoon performed a one-step attachment of soft tissues, tendons, and ligaments to bone during surgical shoulder repair procedures, of which an estimated 300,000 are carried out annually in the United States. Prior to the development of this device, soft tissue reattachment procedures were extremely complex and time consuming. The surgeon was required to make large incisions, drill curved holes, and thread sutures through the bone to attach ligaments. Many of the difficulties and complications associated with those procedures were avoided with the new device.[53]

Meanwhile, market analysts were following Biomet with excitement. Syndicated financial columnist Malcolm Berko once again spotlighted Biomet in a column: "Biomet is an enormously impressive player in the orthopedic devices market,

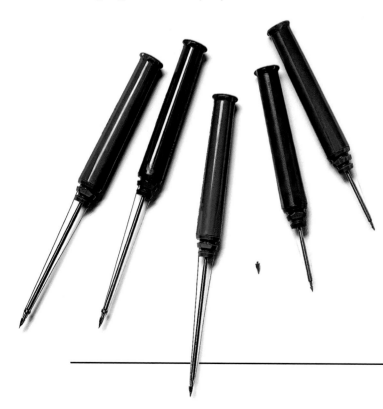

The Harpoon Suture Anchor was designed to more quickly and efficiently attach soft tissues, tendons, and ligaments to bone during surgical shoulder repair procedures.

owning 11 percent of the action. And its record of revenues and earnings since 1982 is awesome with a capital 'A.'"

Regulatory Restraints

The U.S. government was a target for criticism in 1993 when Dane Miller joined four other Hoosier business leaders at Manchester College for a panel discussion on global economics. While the group lauded the opportunities of world markets and endorsed the North American Free Trade Agreement (NAFTA), the attitude toward the federal government was dour. The panel agreed that the United States would not be able to efficiently compete in the international market unless regulation, legislation, and litigation were stemmed.

"Government needs to get out of the way of American business and let American business see what they can do," Miller said. "One of our major problems is the burdens created by our own government."[54]

Health Care Reform

After more than a decade of steady, phenomenal growth across the entire orthopedic industry, the winds of change began to blow. Since the 1980s, health care costs had been increasing by almost 15 percent a year, driving up the cost of insurance and causing millions of Americans to forgo expensive coverage. By the 1990s, the steadily rising costs of health care were destabilizing the nation's medical industry.

In his successful 1991 presidential campaign, Bill Clinton proposed universal health coverage for Americans and cost controls to keep the expense of health care in line.

By late 1993, politicians and political pundits were all eyeing the nation's capital in anticipation of Clinton's much-hyped plan, which promised to overhaul the nation's health care delivery system. Details of the plan were to be released by the president to the U.S. Congress and the public in September.

At the heart of the plan were two issues: universal medical coverage and the government's role in administering that coverage. All citizens would be issued a "health-security card" to ensure they were covered, whether they changed jobs or became ill or unemployed. The new system also called for the creation of a new regulatory hierarchy, including a National Health Board.

While Clinton's proposal addressed an apparent national need, it also threatened to upset an entire industry. The new program would mandate how physicians and hospitals were paid, imposing limits and perhaps forcing doctors to become involved in Health Maintenance Organizations (HMOs). Health plans would be required to meet federal standards for solvency. Physicians and hospitals would not be permitted to bill individuals for unpaid claims. Plans whose proposed premiums exceeded allowed rates would be required to accept lower premiums, and health plan providers would have to adjust payment rates or accept lower profits to make up the difference.

While no successful bill to reform health care ever came out of the debate, the effort coincided with a fundamental change in health care delivery in the United States. HMOs began to multiply. These new mass insurers cut costs by signing up large numbers of people and used bargaining power with hospitals and doctors to keep prices down. Concurrently, the HMOs imposed guidelines on their members, dictating such things as which doctors could be visited, which diagnostics were covered, and how long people could stay in the hospital.

This political climate introduced a number of uncertainties for Biomet and the health care industry in general.

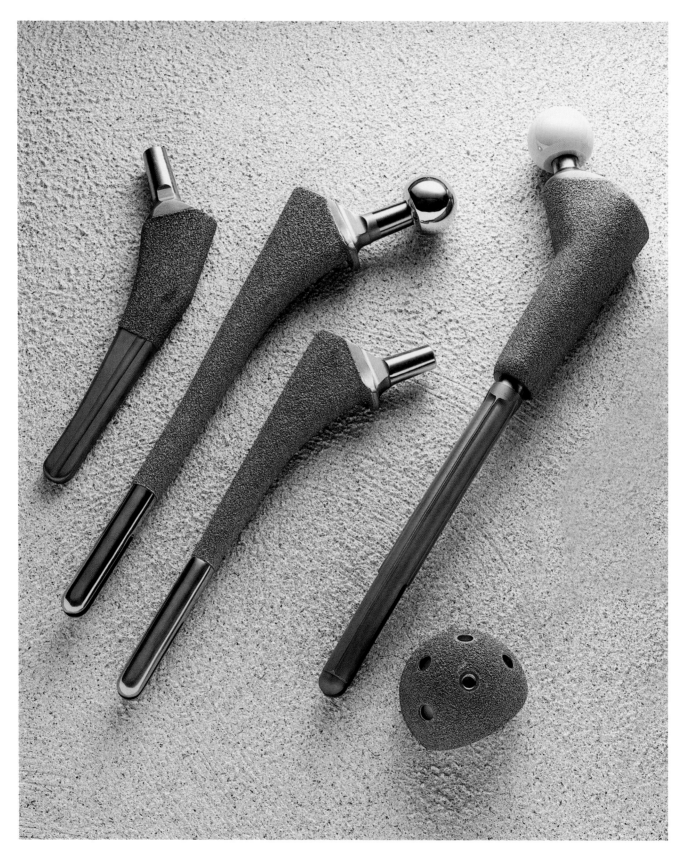

Examples of Biomet hip replacement components in 1995. Biomet offers the broadest total hip product line in the industry and more FDA-approved cementless hips than any competitor.

CHAPTER SIX

PRICING PRESSURES

1994–1995

Dane would rather fight for a surgeon's right to use a competitor's product than to force a surgeon to use Biomet.

—Eric Martin, director of corporate sales, 2001

A S IT EVOLVED FROM A START-up company into one of the orthopedic industry's main suppliers, Biomet did more than simply grow: It took market share away from the established leaders.[1]

This shift took place against the backdrop of a rapidly expanding industry awash in competitive forces. When Biomet entered the orthopedic industry, four large companies dominated the market. By 1994, nearly a dozen orthopedic suppliers had a measurable national market share. And while market-share figures in the orthopedic industry are often a matter of debate, most 1994 estimates put Biomet fourth, holding somewhere between 12 and 14 percent of the overall market.[2]

By the mid-1990s, however, after a period of boom, the orthopedics industry had begun to change, and some industry watchers were raising their eyebrows at Biomet's determined reliance on technological innovation and independent sales reps.[3]

The New Health Care

Suffering under the cost pressures brought on by managed care, hospitals began to study the high costs of their implant programs. In turn, orthopedic companies began to question the very principles they had based themselves on in the 1980s—from the strong role of the surgeons in product selection, to the value of independent sales reps, to the feasibility of continued aggressive product innovation. Within a few years, the orthopedics industry looked like a very different market.[4]

Biomet, however, never seriously questioned its core principles. As Dane Miller and Niles Noblitt wrote in the 1994 annual report, "The domestic orthopedic market growth rate is retracting somewhat with an anticipated calendar year 1994 growth rate of 6 percent to $3.31 billion. Despite some industry trends in cutting research and development expenditures in response to health care reform efforts, Biomet believes this is the wrong course of action and continues to pursue research, development, and new technologies with vigor."[5]

This confidence in the growth of orthopedic reconstructive surgery was based upon another set of numbers. The U.S. population 75 and older was set to increase 25 percent to nearly 19 million by the year 2010. Of these 19 million, 38 percent of males and 63 percent of females could be affected by arthritis.[6]

Cover of the 1994 annual report. Sales increased 11 percent that year, reaching $373.3 million.

Instead of cutting back, Biomet looked for different ways to prosper in a cost-cutting environment dominated by institutional buying groups. One of the company's techniques was the establishment of the Large Account Management Program (LAMP, which later became known as the Health Care Initiatives Program). Looking closely at all costs, the LAMP group worked with hospitals and surgeons to develop cost-effective and efficient orthopedic programs.[7]

Another response was the company's increased reliance on advanced imaging and manufacturing techniques like Computer Assisted Design (CAD) and Computer Assisted Manufacturing (CAM). Since the early 1990s, Biomet had used a process called rapid prototyping, a three-dimensional imaging technique that helped engineers "see" the parts they were creating in great detail before actually making them.

Biomet won the 1994 Challenge Cup, in which Warsaw area industries compete in sports such as track, horseshoes, golf, and basketball. Biomet team members, from left (kneeling), Randa Brandon, Crystal Holbrook, and Janie Rhodes; (standing) Teresa Spangle, Steve Allen, Matt Gaff, Chuck Niemier, Robyn Lamle, David Worland, Dane Miller, Rob Cripe, Melvin Hawkins, and Warsaw Chamber of Commerce President Rob O'Brien.

(Rapid prototyping was also critical in the Patient-Matched Implants department.)

"Cost is critical in our marketplace," Biomet Engineering Services Manager John Amber told *Computer-aided Engineering* magazine. "We have to continue to create profit for our shareholders in an environment where everyone is trying to hold down costs."[8]

Whatever approach Biomet used to contain it, cost pressure, and its close cousin, pricing pressure, would become a standard feature of the orthopedic industry—a development that turned the industry from a profitable one into a business that was difficult to manage.[9]

Bad Medicine

By the mid-1990s, for the first time in their existence, orthopedic companies found themselves competing on the basis of price rather than quality. When asked in 1999 how the industry had changed, CEO Dane Miller responded, "This is certainly a much different market than it was 10 years ago. Back then, no one cared about price. Competition in the industry was based purely on who could come up with the newest technological bell and whistle, provided it had some scientific and clinical basis."[10]

In the new climate, everybody was involved in the pricing game. "The single biggest change [was that] the average orthopedic surgeon today knows how much his hospital is paying for implants and, in some cases, has been an unwilling participant in trying to pressure orthopedic companies for a better price," Miller said. "Unfortunately, in many cases, this industry has allowed itself to be convinced that we're dealing in a commodity marketplace and that all that matters now is price."[11]

According to Miller, sales strategies based upon price fail for two reasons. First, low prices prevent suppliers from offering the support services that are essential to the product's use. For example, Miller recalled a day he was in a Philadelphia hospital that had scheduled several procedures using Biomet implants. "We had a well-trained technical field rep in the operating room from 6 in the morning to 5 in the afternoon," said Miller. "That's an important component of what we

deliver. It may not be in the box, but it's part of what the hospital is buying from us."[12]

The second reason price discounting is a losing strategy is that the company's products are really worth more. "If you look at 10-year clinical results, I think we can prove that our products are better, and that's a message we've stuck with," he said.[13]

Miller recalled a "price-pounding discussion" with a materials manager who was trying to con-

President and CEO Dane Miller, left, and Chairman of the Board Niles Noblitt have provided leadership and inspiration at Biomet since its 1977 incorporation.

vince Miller to sell him Biomet implants at the same prices as the other suppliers had agreed to. "Finally, he said to me, 'You're the only company

Vice President of Marketing William Kolter said some Biomet salespeople were blocked from entering hospitals when the company refused to participate in squeezing surgeons out of the decision-making process in the early days of managed health care.

not willing to meet our price cap,'" Miller said. "I resisted the temptation to respond, 'That's because those other companies may see their products as commodities. We don't.'"[14]

While no health care reform bill had emerged from Washington, health care changed anyway, with far-reaching effects. Physicians, who had worried that Clinton's plan would narrow their influence, found themselves heading into the mid-1990s with vastly reduced power. In their stead, institutional purchasing organizations demanded discounted prices in exchange for a guaranteed market share, remembered Bill Kolter, vice president of marketing.[15]

We said, "Well, how are you going to do that?" They said they'd make the doctors use our product or those that are on the contract—typically one or two or three companies. We said, "You're going to make the doctors do that? How?" They said, "Trust us, we can do it. If the doctors decide not to play ball, we can refuse to sterilize their instruments, revoke their privileges, give them unfavorable operating room time. There are things we can do to basically coerce the doctors to use your implants." We said, "Okay. You want us to be a party to coercing our best friends into using our products?"

Not only is that bad marketing, but that's bad medicine. You know, if we defined our job as selling as many boxes of implants as possible, we probably would have jumped all over those contracts. That's not how we define our job here.[16]

Instead, Biomet continued to advocate surgeon choice, said Eric Martin. "The last thing we want is a surgeon using our products because he's told to . . . and not because he wants to."[17]

When Biomet refused to participate in efforts to dictate which products to use based solely on price, hospitals were not happy.

"Some organizations actually attempted to block our salespeople from entering the hospital," Kolter said.[18]

Bucking the System

The Biomet team continued to develop new approaches to this new price sensitivity. They began aggressively marketing clinical results and developing value-added programs to help physicians and surgeons.

"Physicians were being demonized, and reimbursement cuts for surgeons were coming," Kolter explained. "They were a target, and with 70 percent of total joints being done under Medicare payment, that's a significant part of our customers' income. We were like a start-up company all over again in 1994 because we were under siege big time. But we chose to put ourselves in that position because strategically and ethically, we felt it was the right thing. The doctor ought to be picking the implant. He is prescribing treatment."[19]

But many of Biomet's competitors embraced the terms and moved in. They introduced more low-level products, aggressively discounted their prices, and quit talking about technology.

"They did all of the things that it wouldn't even occur to us to do," Kolter added. "There was such a dichotomy between our approach and everybody else's that it was scaring us a little bit. We're thinking, 'We're either right or we're dead.' I have to give credit to the management of this company. It was a bold move for us to basically thumb our nose at what seemed to be a market trend."[20]

During that time, Biomet's market share rose, and its competitors' dropped.[21]

Growing and Consolidating

Despite the changes in health care—or perhaps because of them—Biomet continued to seek opportunity wherever it was available. In early 1994, the company entered into a bidding war for the right to buy Kirschner Medical Corporation.

Kirschner, a developer, manufacturer, and distributor of products for orthopedic applications, was headquartered in Timonium, Maryland. The firm's orthopedic implant manufacturing facilities were in Fair Lawn, New Jersey, and its soft-goods facilities were in Marlow, Oklahoma, and Delray Beach, Florida. Kirschner also operated international orthopedic manufacturing and sales support facilities in Valencia, Spain.[22]

By May 1994, Kirschner had signed a letter of intent to merge with Orthomet, of Minneapolis. One month later, however, Biomet upset the deal with a larger offer, $35 million, for Kirschner. When Biomet made its offer, Jim Howie, director of corporate development and communications for Biomet, told the business press, "The jury is out."

I'm not convinced that Orthomet's is a better bid. If you are Kirschner, you have to decide if you want

Kirschner's Performance Knee System, as well as other reconstructive devices and soft goods, added depth to Biomet's product portfolio when Kirschner was acquired in 1994.

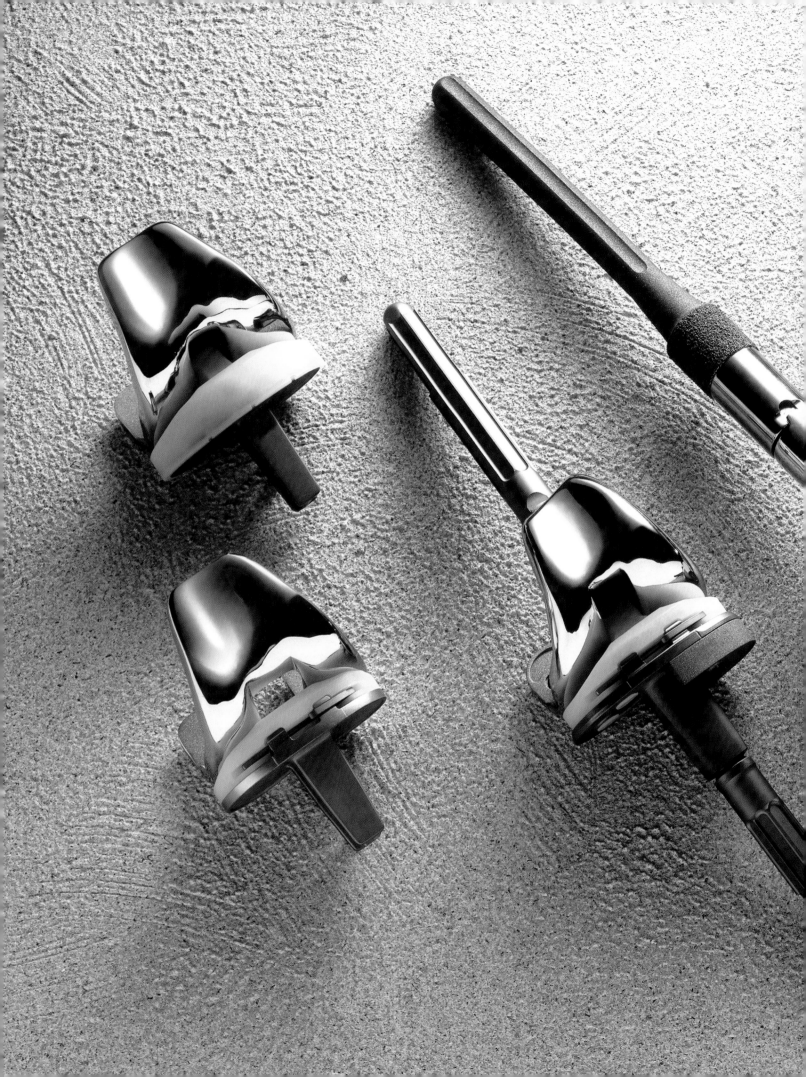

Examples of Biomet's line of reconstructive knee systems in 1995. Biomet's line of knee and hip implants addresses not only the primary market segment but also the rapidly growing revision market.

HUNGRY FOR KNOWLEDGE

THE 1990S OPENED THE DOORWAY to the World Wide Web. Biomet was the first orthopedic company to use this avenue to educate its potential patients.

"We were the first orthopedic company to have a home page that provided information, not only for surgeons and for our sales force, but also for patients encountering some type of orthopedic difficulty," said Lance Perry, director of marketing for knee reconstruction.[1]

In fact, the Web site was selected by an independent panel to receive the Six Senses of Approval award, sponsored by ECHO Strategies Group of Boston, in 1996. The award was available to only the medical and health care industries.[2]

The goals of Biomet's site were to inform the patient about what happens in a given procedure and what technologies are involved, and to help people make decisions that are best for them, Perry added.[3]

That access to information has created a more educated and interested public, said Paula Hoesel, corrective action coordinator. "It's amazing to see, over the last couple of years, how much patients get directly involved in their health care," she said. "They seek us out, want to know what this device is, what its track record is. They're information hungry."[4]

ately after this announcement, Kirschner received yet another offer, this time from Maxxim Medical, in Texas. Maxxim and Kirschner already had a history; the two firms had been in merger discussions in 1993, but Kirschner had pulled out.

This time, Maxxim offered to trade three shares of its stock, which had recently closed at $15.50, for every two shares of Kirschner stock, or to pay $10.85 in cash per share, at Kirschner's discretion. Considered against Biomet's offer of 1.01 shares for every Kirschner share—and considering that Maxxim was "one of the fastest growing public companies in the United States"[24]—the new offer caused Kirschner's board of directors to pause.

Biomet, however, had no intention of being squeezed out of an attractive deal. A day after Maxxim's offer came in, Biomet counteroffered with .9 share of Biomet stock in exchange for each share of Kirschner, or $10.75 in cash, at Kirschner's discretion.

Although Biomet's offer was still lower than Maxxim's, Kirschner soon announced a definitive agreement to merge with Biomet. Kirschner spurned the higher offer for a variety of reasons, according to analysts. Aaron Shackelford, vice president at Principal Financial Securities, in Dallas, cited the failed attempt to merge two years before. "They didn't end on positive terms," he told *Warfield's Business Record.*[25] More important, however, were the potential advantages to both Biomet and Kirschner. Kevin Morrow, a health care products analyst with The Ohio Company, called the acquisition "a great move" since Kirschner would add depth to Biomet's product line.

Kirschner CEO C. Scott Harrison, M.D., described Biomet's offer as "friendly" and remarked, "There was a lot more certainty with Biomet."[26]

to go with a $25-million-a-year company who may be trying to find a way to survive in the market, or go with one of the world's largest orthopedic companies, who is trying to acquire them in a nonhostile manner.[23]

Within a few weeks, Kirschner's board of directors made its choice: it accepted Biomet's offer. Yet the drama was far from over. Almost immedi-

Retired President and Chief Executive Officer of Kirschner Medical Corporation C. Scott Harrison, M.D., still sits on Biomet's board.

Kirschner offered a varied product line that complemented and added depth to Biomet's product portfolio. Its orthopedic division produced joint replacements for hips, knees, and shoulders, as well as spinal implants and fracture fixation products.[27] Indeed, at the time of the acquisition, Kirschner was the market leader in shoulder implants.[28] Another top product was Kirschner's Performance Knee System. With 10 years of design history and six years of successful follow-up studies, the Performance Knee was designed to provide the stability needed for ligament and soft tissue support.[29]

Kirschner's soft-goods division offered braces, supports, splints, and cast materials used to support, or postoperatively treat, the body's musculoskeletal structures.[30] The division's highest-volume product line was synthetic casting tape.[31]

On November 4, Biomet completed the acquisition of Kirschner, paying $39.9 million for about 3.5 million shares.[32] In a related move, Biomet also purchased Figgie International's entire 685,222-share stake in Kirschner (representing 19.9 percent of outstanding shares) and a $2.5 million promissory note from Kirschner's Spanish subsidiary.[33]

At the end of 1994, Biomet once again reported record sales, net income, and earnings per share. It was the 16th consecutive year of increases in both revenues and net income.[34] Sales increased 11 percent to $373.3 million. The company's U.S.-based revenue grew 12 percent to $288.2 million, while international sales increased 9 percent to $85.1 million. International sales were negatively affected by a stronger U.S. dollar relative to the British pound.[35]

The company's worldwide reconstructive device sales that year were $218.1 million, which represented a 15 percent increase. The growth was due largely to the Maxim Total Knee System, introduced in late 1993.

Sales of EBI's products grew 8 percent to $88.7 million.[36] This increase was largely due to increased demand for electrical stimulation products, which included a smaller, lighter, and user-friendly Bone Healing System—Model 1200. The new system represented a complete redesign to encourage patient compliance in the treatment of nonunion fractures, a strategy which in turn enhanced clinical success.[37]

Biomet's "other products" category totaled $66.4 million, which represented a 3 percent increase over 1993, primarily as a result of increased sales of Arthrotek's IES 1000 System and Lorenz's oral-maxillofacial implants.[38]

Research and development expenses rose from 5.4 percent of sales in 1993 to 5.5 percent in 1994, reflecting Biomet's commitment to sustain its edge through technological advancements.[39]

In September 1993, the company's board of directors authorized the repurchase of up to $25 million of the issued and outstanding common shares of the company in either open market or privately negotiated purchases. By the end of its 1994 fiscal year on May 31, Biomet had repurchased nearly 1.3 million shares of its common stock at a total cost of $12.3 million.[40]

Success in Uncertain Times

In 1995 the ongoing challenges presented by managed health care created uncertainty for patients and providers. While patients postponed procedures, expecting a change in the delivery of service, hospitals cut back on their purchases of capital equipment.[41] In addition, cost containment concerns caused health care providers to become more selective in the use of high-cost reconstructive devices, which were increasingly being limited to younger, more active patients.[42]

Despite all the changes that took place in 1995, Biomet continued to capture market share due to aggressive marketing, its firm focus on research and development, and the Kirschner Medical Corporation acquisition.[43] When Biomet closed its books for 1995, it registered its 17th consecutive year of increases in both revenue and net income.[44] Sales increased 21 percent to $452.3 million, while net income rose 13 percent to $79.2 million.[45]

The company's U.S.-based revenue grew 19 percent to $343.8 million, while foreign sales jumped 27 percent to $108.5 million. EBI's sales increased 11 percent to $98.5 million. With the inclusion of seven months of revenue from Kirschner's soft-goods division, sales in Biomet's "other products" category jumped 22 percent to $81.1 million.[46]

As Biomet's sales rose, so did a need for some expansion at Lorenz Surgical.[47] After being acquired, Lorenz had established limited manufacturing operations in Warsaw, Indiana, and quickly added new products. By 1995, however, it was decided that Lorenz would benefit from moving the entire operation back to Jacksonville.

"There was a contingent of people in Warsaw who made up the Lorenz room," remembered Jerry Ferguson, who had been managing Lorenz since its acquisition. "Those people all transferred down to Jacksonville."[48]

As operations transferred, Biomet drew up expansion plans, and in late 1995 it broke

ground for a two-story, 66,000-square-foot manufacturing plant adjacent to the existing Jacksonville building. The new structure was to house all of the subsidiary's manufacturing and engineering operations as well as administrative offices for accounting, customer service, and sales.[49]

Opposite: Biomet's Warsaw facility obtained ISO 9001 certification in 1994 for meeting international quality standards for products sold in Europe. From left are Manager of Regulatory Affairs John Wagoner, Dane Miller, Director of Regulatory Affairs Patty Beres, and Director of Quality Assurance Rex White.

Right: Biomet team members wished President and CEO Dane Miller a happy 48th birthday in 1994. The plane on the cake represents Miller's Beachcraft King Air.

Below: The 1994 board of directors and officers included (seated from left) Greg Hartman, Dan Hann, Niles Noblitt, Marilyn Tucker Quayle, Dave Montgomery, and Ken Miller; and (standing from left) Jerry Miller, Gene Tanner, Garry England, Anthony Fleming, Charles Niemier, Dane Miller, James Norris, Joel Pratt, Jerry Ferguson, Ray Harroff, and Thomas Kearns Jr.

Biomet's worldwide sales of reconstructive devices, such as these hip and knee components, reached $352.1 million during fiscal year 1997.

CHAPTER SEVEN

PROTECTING ASSETS

1996–1997

*Part of the reason Biomet team members stay with us is because they
are empowered in their jobs and they have incredible opportunities for
advancement.*

—Darlene Whaley, vice president of human resources, 2001

IN 1996, BIOMET CELEBRATED a milestone of maturity: After long years of piling profit back into the growth-hungry company, the board of directors issued Biomet's first dividend. The dividend of 10 cents a share was announced by company CEO Dane Miller at the annual meeting.

"Until the decision to pay the dividend, Biomet retained its earnings to pay for acquisitions or finance research efforts on the theory it could provide a greater return for shareholders in that manner," reported the *South Bend Tribune*. With its first dividend, Biomet expected to distribute about $11.5 million to shareholders.[1]

It was an important occasion—one that marked Biomet's 18th consecutive year of climbing revenue and income. Sales in 1996 increased 18 percent, to $535.2 million from $452.3 million.[2]

Once again, it was sales within the reconstructive device product category that led the way. Worldwide sales in this category increased 20 percent to $326.8 million, while EBI's devices recorded sales of $108.6 million, an increase of 10 percent. Sales of the company's "other products" grew 23 percent to $99.7 million.[3]

The year's 28 percent increase in international sales came after several years of effort to strengthen Biomet's position in Europe. The company began to develop France, Germany, Italy, and Spain, in addition to the United Kingdom, as "home" markets. From its Warsaw, Indiana, roots, strong branches had grown in Europe.[4]

In 1996, Biomet Europe was established to coordinate European activities and to maximize the company's manufacturing and distribution resources. Sales, development, and manufacturing operations were set up in Germany, Spain, and the United Kingdom, while France and Italy served as sales centers.[5]

Paving the way for further international product expansion, Biomet's Warsaw facility obtained ISO 9002 certification during 1996. The facility met international quality standards for products sold in the European Community and was therefore able to place the "CE" mark on its manufactured products, allowing sales without further regulatory barriers.[6]

Products introduced during 1996 included the AGC HPS Posterior-Stabilized Knee, the AGC Universal V-2, the DynaFix External Fixation

Darlene Whaley, vice president of human resources, has seen the number of team members at the Warsaw facility triple since she came to Biomet in 1988.

Above: Illustration of the DynaFix External Fixation System, the market leader in the United States. Biomet successfully launched this product through its EBI subsidiary in 1996.

Left: Biomet's Universal Ringloc and Rx90 Ringloc acetabular components helped drive 1996 sales to $535.2 million.

was a porous-coated conical cup with fins to help hold it in place.[10]

After Tronzo developed his system, Biomet began selling a hip replacement system that contained a hemispherical cup with fins and a proprietary porous coating—the Mallory-Head system—which Tronzo claimed was too similar to his own.[11] However, Biomet's system was developed by two other doctors, William Head and Tom Mallory. As Biomet's defense attorney, Martin Reeder, said, "The patent which Tronzo sought to enforce was based on an old idea that goes back to the 1950s."[12] Nonetheless, a jury in West Palm Beach County, Florida, found that the patent was valid and had been infringed and awarded Tronzo a total of $55.5 million.[13]

Although it was a large judgment—especially considering that the product in question accounted for less than 1 percent of Biomet's annual sales—analysts were quick to point out that it would probably not damage the company permanently. Analyst David Lebedeff, with NatCity Investments, in Indianapolis, told the *South Bend Tribune* that Biomet had the cash reserves—a fact that likely attracted lawsuits.

"People don't sue people who don't have money," Lebedeff remarked. "When you have a lot of money sitting around, and [Biomet is] a profitable company, you're probably going to be the target of lawsuits."[14]

Tellingly, Biomet's stock didn't suffer too badly. The price dropped from around $20 a share to $18, and First of Michigan downgraded the shares from a "buy" to a "hold," but only because Biomet's stock had reached a high.[15]

Fortunately, the complete judgment did not stand. In August 1998, the U.S. Court of Appeals struck down the jury award. The appellate court accepted Biomet's position on all the patent issues and found Tronzo's patent claims to be invalid and therefore uninfringeable. The appellate court did, however, remand the case to the district court for further consideration on the state law claims only, which limited Tronzo's ability to recover damages.

In the summer of 1999, the appellate court panel unanimously remanded the case and ordered the district judge to ascertain damages by reviewing the existing record or gathering

System, the Precept Total Hip System, the Vision Total Hip System, and the Mallory-Head Modular Calcar Hip.[7] The Calcar Hip, a member of the Mallory-Head Modular Calcar Revision series, was designed to provide customized fixation alternatives in difficult hip revision cases. In combination with easy-to-use, quick-connect Mallory-Head modular instrumentation, it made a higher level of surgical precision possible.[8]

The Litigation Story

On January 25, 1996, Biomet announced a jury verdict in a lawsuit by orthopedic surgeon Dr. Raymond Tronzo in the District Court for the Southern District of Florida.[9]

In 1984, Tronzo had developed a hip replacement system for which he received a patent in 1988. One component of the system new evidence. District Judge Daniel Hurley declined to seek new evidence and ruled that Tronzo was entitled to compensatory damages of $520—his patent filing fee—and punitive damages of $50,000. Furthermore, Judge Hurley even went on to say, "I would have ruled for Biomet had I been the trier of fact."[16]

A decision regarding the state law claims was reached on January 18, 2001, when the U.S. Court of Appeals reinstated $20 million in punitive damages awarded as part of the original jury verdict. This decision was based on a technical point, not on the facts of the case; apparently, the court argued, Biomet had waived the issue of punitive damages.

Biomet sought a review of the case by the United States Supreme Court. During the third quarter of fiscal 2001, even before the Supreme Court had decided whether to accept the case, the company recorded a one-time special charge of $26.1 million, including interest and related expenses, in connection with the damages award.[17] In November 2001, the Supreme Court refused to hear the case, allowing the award of $20 million in punitive damages to stand.[18]

Daniel Hann, senior vice president and general counsel, said the ultimate decision was an unfortunate one in that it reverberated through the legal media. While the Supreme Court was still considering Biomet's writ of certiorari, an article was published in the *National Law Journal* criticizing the circuit court's decision to reinstate the $20 million punitive damage award.[19]

Although the punitive damage award would have no effect on Biomet's stock or operations, it was still a personal blow to a company that had suffered relatively little litigation in a very litigious industry. In general, the number of claims against Biomet compared to other companies with its volume of sales has generally been minimal, said Brad Tandy, assistant general counsel and corporate compliance officer.

There are a lot of patents in the field, and it's always a challenge to make certain you're not infringing on anyone else's property rights while also watching your own property rights. Whether or not there are others out there not respecting your rights is something that you
have to constantly monitor. We are a company that would rather compete in the marketplace than in the courtroom.[20]

Sharing Growth

Litigation was a fact of life in the medical industry, but Biomet's idea of the marketplace was much more human, based on patient care and empowered team members.

These high-tech elements found in Biomet products have brought the company resounding success. Its clinically proven and cost-effective technology is often attributed to the engineering background of the company's founders and their high level of insight into new technologies.

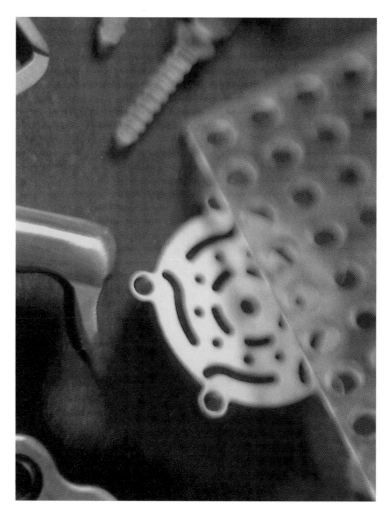

Throughout the years, the company has participated in charitable activities both locally and nationally. In March 1996, Lorenz Surgical carried Biomet's generosity into the international arena when it set out to play a significant role in a medical mission to Guatemala.

Through a donation of surgical instruments and plating systems, Lorenz was part of a team of medical professionals who performed approximately 120 surgical procedures, medical evaluations, and treatments. The subsidiary worked in partnership with the HELPS International organization, which coordinates donations for such medical missions of mercy.[21]

Later that year, on September 13, 1996, Lorenz finally became a fully integrated company after opening its 60,000-square-foot manufacturing addition to its Jacksonville, Florida, facility.[22]

Pre-Operative   Pre-Operative

Post-Operative   Post-Operative

Above: This Guatemalan boy's face was successfully transformed with the help of a mid-face distractor. Designed by Martin Chin, D.D.S., and Bryant Toth, M.D., the product was manufactured by Biomet subsidiary Lorenz Surgical. The boy was one of many whose lives were touched by Biomet's HELPS partnership in 1996.

Left: These distractors and plates are used to transform the facial bones and generate bone growth. Lorenz distraction technology is used for challenging mandibular, or jawbone, and mid-face treatments in pediatric and adult patients.

Clockwise from top are the mid-face distractor, the pediatric mandibular distractor, and two examples of linear mandibular distractors. The pediatric distractor is used in children up to 16 years of age who may exhibit severe asymmetry, underdeveloped jawbone, and/or airway obstruction. The linear distractor is used for posttraumatic defects and bone loss after treatment of tumors.

BIOMET ON WHEELS

IN THE MID-1990S THE BIOMET LOGO zoomed before the eyes of sports spectators when the company began sponsoring racecars in Indianapolis. The logo, emblazoned on a nose cone here and a quarter panel there, did more than just broaden Biomet's public visibility.

Lyn St. James, often the only female driver in a race and only the second woman ever to compete at Indianapolis, recalled the beginning of her relationship with Biomet. "When I lost my sponsor at Indianapolis in 1995, Dane Miller was the first person I contacted who said 'yes' to a sponsorship proposal. I'll never forget that."[1]

Biomet team members got to know drivers and attended many of the races. Customers also enjoyed perks; the company arranged track tours for visiting orthopedic surgeons. Miller said there were times St. James spent two hours showing the doctors around the track and discussing racing at the Indianapolis Motor Speedway.

More recently, Miller's wife, Mary Louise, bought a Pontiac racecar. But although the car bears the Biomet name, the company does not sponsor it or support it financially. It is driven in races all over the country in the Automobile Racing Club of America circuit by such drivers as Jason Jarrett. Mary Louise's unlikely hobby and her company, ML Motorsports, began when her son-in-law worked with a racing team in Florida in the late 1990s. He came back and planted the idea in her head.

"I decided for some unknown reason to form a little corporation," Mary Louise said. "Dane didn't really know we were so serious about it. But now he is our best supporter—our biggest fan." He often serves as a spotter. One of Mary Louise's favorite things about owning a race car is getting others excited about it. "We do a lot of entertaining with our doctors [through Biomet] at the track, and I've had so many [doctors'] wives say to me, 'I didn't want to come, and I didn't think I was going to like it, but I loved it!' Now they are watching racing on television," she said.

"I used to think it was ridiculous the way they drove in circles," Mary Louise said. "But when you actually get to the track, it gets your blood moving. It's a whole different story once you understand racing and understand the engineering it takes to do this."[2]

Biomet founder Jerry Ferguson takes the ML Motorsports Pontiac for a spin in the parking lot at Biomet headquarters. The car, owned by Mary Louise Miller, bears the Biomet name.

Bill Hartman (left), product manager for knees, and Michael Armstrong (right), international marketing manager, demonstrate a knee replacement system during surgeon tours of the Warsaw facility.

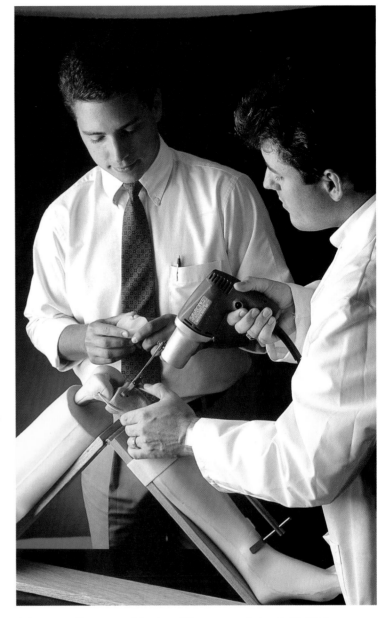

The 20th Anniversary

As 1997 drew to a close, it was a good time to take stock of Biomet's first twenty years (the company was actually incorporated in 1977, although the first year of business was 1978). That anniversary year, Biomet's annual report contained a record of the company's financial history—from sales of $17,000 in 1978 to 1997's sales of $580 million. Net income in 1997 grew 13 percent to $106.5 million.[23]

The company's sales growth was due mostly to its penetration of the reconstructive device market. While the market in the United States remained competitive, issues of pricing began to stabilize, and the industry began to concentrate more on the quality of care than its cost alone.[24] Biomet's worldwide sales of reconstructive devices increased 8 percent during 1997, reaching $352.1 million.[25] The products that contributed the most to this growth were the Maxim Total Knee and Alliance Hip systems.[26]

EBI's sales continued to increase. The subsidiary's sales force also swelled—from approximately 118 in 1993 to nearly 225 in 1997. Indeed, these strategies allowed EBI to grow from $50.7 million in sales in 1990 to $114.3 million in 1997.

The company's "other product" sales—which included Lorenz Surgical, internal fixation systems, Arthrotek, and other products—jumped 14 percent to $113.9 million.[27]

Biomet's overall international sales during 1997 increased close to 12 percent to $154.8 million. The greatest sales growth came about in Europe, Latin America, and the Pacific Rim.[28]

Throughout this rapid growth, Biomet had gone from a handful of founders working in a converted barn to a global company with 2,500 team members. The original barn was vacated and the company moved into headquarters in Warsaw that would steadily expand to 345,000 square feet by the turn of the century.

Beyond the Numbers

But the numbers alone tell only part of the story. As it had transitioned from soft goods into reconstructive devices and implants, Biomet had made a lasting contribution to the medical industry. From its early innovations—such as titanium alloy, compression molded polyethylene, and plasma spray porous coating—to its gold-standard products—for example, the Maxim Total Knee and Mallory-Head Total Hip—Biomet had compiled a record of flexible innovation. It was a company clearly devoted to the best possible patient outcomes.

Behind each of Biomet's implants lay a story. The company's 1997 newsletter, *Bio Briefs*, spotlighted Rick Cooper, who was driving on Chicago's Edens Expressway in early 1994 when he was struck by a car involved in a high-speed police chase. In the accident, Cooper's left elbow was "basically shattered," an injury that would likely have resulted in amputation.

Cooper, however, was lucky. Instead of amputating, his doctors chose a bone graft. A year after the accident, when it became apparent the bone graft wasn't taking, his physician, Dr. Martin Greenburg, at Illinois Masonic Hospital, ordered an EBI Bone Growth Stimulator. But it turned out

bone stimulation wouldn't work because of the severity of Cooper's injuries.

Soon he and his wife contacted Biomet directly and found out that Biomet made an elbow device but that because of FDA restrictions, it had not been approved for sale in the United States yet. Cooper was directed to Dr. Joseph Pooley in the United Kingdom, who worked closely with Biomet engineers to develop an elbow device.

In 1997, 43 Biomet team members raised $950 in a Bowlathon to help colleague Trent Sutton pay medical expenses when he suffered a severe spinal cord injury. From left are Mark Hamilton, Deb McIntire, Deb Gilliam (of Gilliam Lanes), Peggy Brock, Steve Anderson, Brad Sutter, and Rob Roberts.

Late in 1995, more than 18 months after the accident, Pooley implanted a custom-made, single-hinge Biomet elbow. By 1997, Cooper had a functioning elbow and had regained use of his arm.

This story, like so many others, is part of the daily routine at Biomet, just one of the thousands of individual reasons the company has attracted a motivated workforce, steadily expanded in its industry, and even been a major influence in its hometown of Warsaw, Indiana. An unlikely town for a major medical industry to choose as its headquarters, Warsaw had benefited greatly from its corporate citizens, including market leaders Biomet, DePuy, Zimmer, and, more recently, Medtronic.

"Replacement hips and knees have been Warsaw's claim to fame since the late 1970s," declared *Indiana Business* magazine in a profile of Biomet's local operations. "The city of Warsaw, a community of 13,000 people, seems to offer the best of the rural and urban lifestyles."[29]

The Biomet joint venture with Merck KGaA brought Septocoll to the wound-healing market. The hemostatic agent is a collagen-based resorbable with Gentamicin antibiotic.

CHAPTER EIGHT

GAINING MOMENTUM

1998–1999

They always took the bull by the horns and got the job done. In my opinion, they had the right mix of expertise.

—Barb Akers, regulatory specialist, 2001

B Y THE LATE 1990S, Biomet's industry was poised on the brink of great change. Throughout the 1990s, cost pressures on health care had rippled throughout the medical industry with far-ranging effects. Not only did this pressure reduce physician choice and squeeze Biomet's prices; it also affected the larger companies in Biomet's field. Faced with hospital buying groups that sought reduced prices in return for guaranteed market share, industry pacesetters felt enormous temptation to achieve economies of scale through mergers.

In 1998, the expected consolidation finally arrived. That November, Johnson & Johnson acquired DePuy in a $3.5 billion transaction, merging its orthopedic business into DePuy's. A month later, Stryker acquired Howmedica from Pfizer in a $1.65 billion transaction. As a result of these mergers among its largest rivals, Biomet saw its market position slip despite its steadily increasing share of the domestic reconstructive device market.

Yet Biomet was not easily intimidated by its much larger competitors. In fact, according to Michael Weinstein, an analyst at J. P. Morgan Securities, there was a silver lining to the industry shake-up. "In the months ahead, Biomet hopes to capitalize on the upheaval in its industry by hiring away leading sales reps, winning new accounts, and increasing market share,"

Weinstein told *Investor's Business Daily*. "While competitors focus on important consolidation issues, such as merging overlapping distribution networks, Biomet must use this time to strengthen its position."[1]

Indeed, Biomet began to rapidly accumulate benefits. According to CEO Dane Miller, Biomet hired 20 salespeople from its competitors within six months of the announced mergers and expected to hire 25 more. "When there are significant changes in the marketplace, some salespeople are always looking for a home," Miller said.[2]

At least for the short term, Weinstein expected Biomet to prosper from the consolidating industry by taking shrewd advantage of disgruntled salespeople and neglected customers while the other companies settled their consolidations.

"[But] what happens to Biomet in two to three years, that's the big question," he remarked. As

---

This unique surgical device, the Indiana Tome Carpal Tunnel Release System, is a patented product sold through Biomet.

competition tightened, Biomet could be expected to "buy some companies down the road."[3]

The Biomet-Merck Force

While never ruling out acquisitions, Biomet had generated its own strategies to deal with industry pressure: promoting large account management, boosting quality and technology, and refusing to bend to commodity pricing.

Over the years, Biomet had also consistently posted outstanding international sales, which sometimes represented as much as 25 percent of its overall revenue picture. In late 1997, Biomet announced plans for a joint venture that would surely boost this figure. Reaching for economies of its own, Biomet had arranged a joint venture with Merck Biomaterial, the orthopedic arm of German pharmaceutical giant Merck KGaA. The 50-50 joint venture, known as Biomet-Merck, became effective on January 1, 1998.[4]

"This organization will be one of the strongest development and marketing groups in the European orthopedic market," Dane Miller announced to the business press. "Access to Merck's superior biomaterial technologies will provide the Biomet group with a wide array of new products flowing well into the next century. We are proud to have been selected as Merck's partner."[5]

Dr. Bernhard Scheuble, deputy member of the executive board of Merck KGaA, agreed that Biomet and his company shared common values and vision.

In Biomet we have a partner who will leverage our strong development capability internationally. The strategic fit between Biomet's European operations and Merck KGaA's Biomaterial division is complementary in terms of product lines, geography, and core competencies. Our partnership with Biomet will provide strong access to the important U.S. market for Biomet-Merck's comprehensive line of existing and future biomaterial products.[6]

The company leaders had every reason to be optimistic; the venture was replete with synergies.

Biomet-Merck's Endobon Hydroxyapatite Bone Substitute material demonstrated 10 years of clinical results, differentiating it from other bone-substitute materials.

Not only was Merck KGaA a leading European orthopedic company, but it also possessed a large business in biological agents and was Europe's leading seller of bone cement. For its participation in the joint venture, Merck KGaA obtained access to the U.S. biomaterials market.[7]

"The combination of Merck's innovative biomaterials product line with Biomet's strong reputation in orthopedics will enable Biomet-Merck to provide a full range of products to orthopedic surgeons in Europe and throughout the world," remarked Niles Noblitt, who was named CEO and managing director of Biomet-Merck.[8]

Biomet became the general partner with a 50 percent interest, and Merck KGaA became a limited partner with a 50 percent interest.[9]

At the time of the joint venture, Biomet already had a solid foundation in Europe. Beginning with OEC and Kirschner, Biomet had assembled a $120 million European business. Merck's operation would add another $80 million, creating a European orthopedics business expected to generate

$200 million in 1999. (This figure represented less than 10 percent of the $2.5 billion orthopedic market in Europe.)

Biomet-Merck is headquartered in Zwijndrecht, the Netherlands, and its research facilities are based in Darmstadt, Germany. Manufacturing facilities are located in Swindon, England; Bridgend, Wales; Valencia, Spain; Valence, France; and Berlin, Germany. In addition, Biomet-Merck maintains distribution facilities in Holland, Belgium, Poland, Italy, Switzerland, Austria, Norway, Greece, Portugal, and Czech Republic. The joint venture's combined sales force consisted of more than 300 sales representatives in 2001 and altogether, Biomet-Merck employed approximately 1,100.[10]

Its products included Merck's existing bone cement, Refobacin Palacos, and Endobon bone substitute. Palacos bone cement was sold in the United States, Canada, and all over Europe. Japan rejected it, however, due to a unique chemical component,[11] said John Wagoner, director of regulatory compliance, adding that Biomet refused to change any product just to boost marketability.

If we did that, it wouldn't be the product it is. In all of these years, never, never has Biomet been willing to compromise the patient in order to get a regulatory approval. That is something that I have an extremely high regard for. I've never

Biobon Bone Substitute is a synthetic calcium phosphate material that can be injected or molded into a graft site.

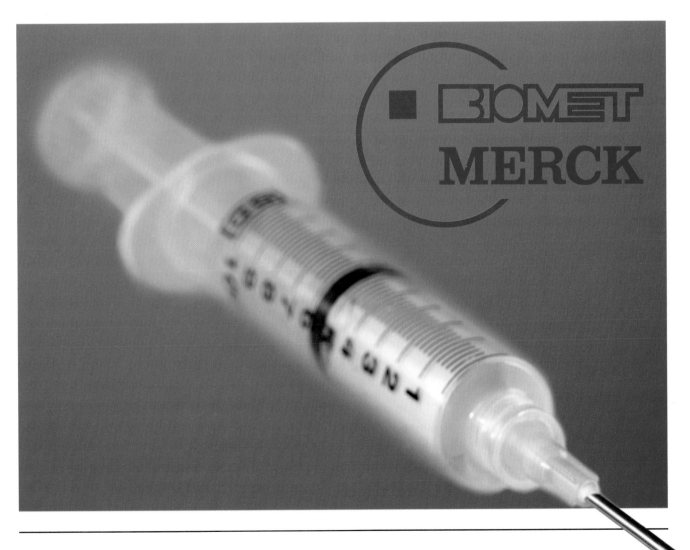

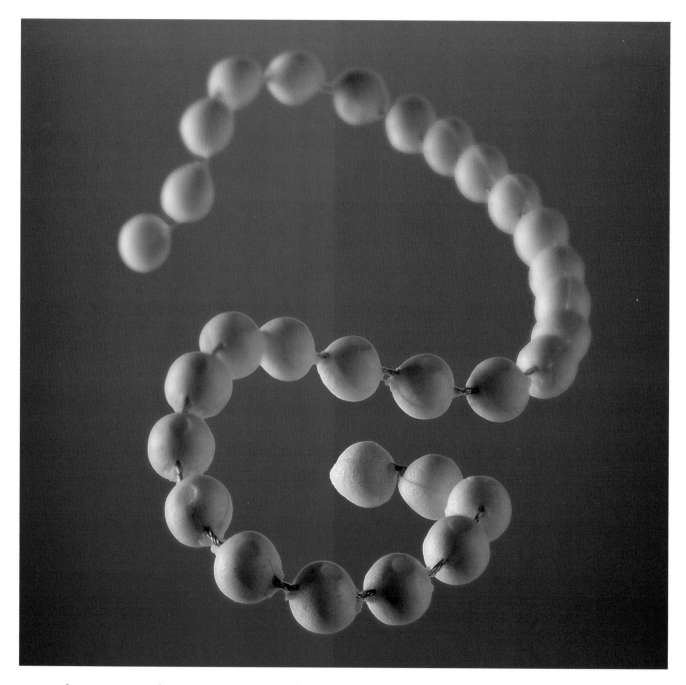

once been pressured to get an approval for a product that wasn't what it should have been.[12]

In the wound-healing area, the joint venture brought to the Canadian market Septopal, an antibiotic bead delivery system used to combat soft tissue infections. Biomet-Merck made Septopal for Biomet in Canada. Biomet-Merck also provided two bone substitute materials to the European marketplace. Endobon, a cancellous bone graft

Septopal is an antibiotic bead delivery system used to combat soft tissue infections. Biomet-Merck made Septopal for Biomet in Canada.

substitute, boasted excellent integration capabilities. The second, Biobon, was a synthetic calcium phosphate material that could be injected or molded into a graft site.[13]

Sustained Innovation

On the domestic front, Biomet unveiled about 40 new products at the 1998 meeting of the American Academy of Orthopaedic Surgeons. These included EBI's SpineLink Cervical Spinal Fixation System, which addressed the cervical section of the spine; the Recovery Protrusio Cage, an acetabular replacement system used in severe revision and oncology situations; Embarc Calcium Phosphate Bone Graft Substitute Material, used in dental and alveolar ridge augmentation procedures; and the Vari-Angle Compression Hip Screw.[14]

By this time, Biomet had become the third-largest manufacturer in the reconstructive device market in the United States. The company's market share had increased from an estimated 6 percent in 1987 to 14 percent by 1998.[15] Driven forward by new products, Biomet posted its 22nd year of record financial gains (because of Biomet's fiscal year, results from Biomet-Merck wouldn't accrue until 1999) with sales of $651.4 million.[16]

The year's reporting of sales was based upon Biomet's realignment of its product lines into four major groups: reconstructive devices, fixation, spinal products, and other products.[17]

The reconstructive device category included total knee, hip, and shoulder systems; bone cements; and the procedure-specific instruments needed to implant Biomet's reconstructive systems. In 1998, reconstructive device sales increased 11 percent to $389.5 million.[18]

Fixation product sales encompassed internal and external fixation devices, craniomaxillofacial fixation systems, and EBI's electrical stimulation devices that did not treat the spine. Sales in this category rose 9 percent to $144.8 million.[19]

Spinal product sales included EBI's SpF Spinal Fusion Stimulation System and the SpineLink, Omega 21, and K2 spinal fixation systems. Sales in this group increased 14 percent to $35.9 million.[20]

The company's "other product" sales category was broadened to include arthroscopy products, soft goods products, casting materials, general surgical instruments, and operating room supplies, as well as unique surgical products, such as the Indiana Tome Carpal Tunnel Release System. This category's sales increased 19 percent to $81.2 million.[21]

Finally, Biomet's international sales increased 21 percent to $187.4 million in 1998.[22] This figure, like Biomet's overall sales, was to rise rapidly in 1999, once the Biomet-Merck joint venture was included in reported results. In fact, international sales jumped 31 percent in 1999, to $246.3 million, and overall sales rose to $827.9 million.[23]

Also in 1999, Biomet opened a new Applied Technology facility in Warsaw, just across the parking lot from headquarters.[24] The original, 10,000-square-foot building had opened in 1992, but by 1999 an updated facility was needed to expand the chemical laboratory and consolidate the research group. A conference room and a six-station cadaver lab were added to the plans, as well as an area to package acrylic bone cements. In May, the doors to a new, 25,000-square-foot building opened.[25]

EBI's SpineLink Intrasegmental Fixation System complements the EBI spinal fusion stimulation line. The market for these procedures is large, with an estimated 238,000 fusions performed in the United States annually.

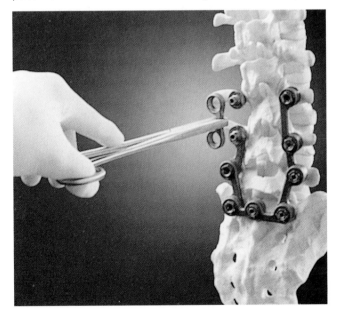

A BRIEF HISTORY OF MERCK

WHILE BIOMET WAS FOUNDED IN 1977, the roots of Merck reach back into the 17th century. In 1668, Friedrich Jacob Merck, an apothecary from Schweinfurt, Germany, assumed ownership of the "Engel-Apotheke," or Angel Pharmacy, in Darmstadt, Germany, and the business has been in the possession of the family ever since. In 1816, Emanuel Merck—the grandson of the Hessian military councilor Johann Heinrich Merck and a friend of Johann Wolfgang Goethe, the famed German poet and dramatist—took over the pharmacy.

Thanks to his scientific education, which was extraordinarily good for that time, his efforts in the pharmacy laboratory in isolating and characterizing alkaloids, a class of highly efficacious vegetable constituents that had been discovered only a short time before, were very successful. He started manufacturing these substances in bulk in 1827 and offered a "Cabinet of Pharmaceutical and Chemical Innovations" for sale that contained all the alkaloids known at the time.

From these humble beginnings in the pharmacy laboratory, he and his successors gradually built up a chemical-pharmaceutical factory that produced—in addition to raw materials for pharmaceutical preparations—a multitude of other fine chemicals and, more recently, ready-to-use medicines. More than 800 individual products were listed in the firm's 1860 catalog. By the turn of the century, the catalog contained roughly 10,000 items. From its very start, Merck was known not only for the diversity of its product range but also for the high degree of purity of its preparations.

When Emanuel Merck died in 1854, the management of the pharmacy and factory was taken over by his sons—Carl, Georg, and Wilhelm—and later on by their descendants. The company grew steadily from 50 employees in 1855 to roughly 1,000 by 1900.

Also by 1900, Merck began exporting its products to several countries. It had also founded subsidiaries throughout the world, setting up large branch offices in London, New York, and Moscow. In 1889, Georg Merck, a grandson of Emanuel Merck, took over the sales office in New York and established Merck & Co. Ten years later he began producing chemicals in the United States.

By the turn of the century, the original Darmstadt location had become too small, so the entire factory was moved to its present site just outside Darmstadt.

Both the workforce and production doubled in the decade before the start of World War I in 1914, but years of raw material shortages and a lack of skilled workers followed. However, the war itself hastened a transition in the pharmaceutical industry to the production of drug specialties. The year 1915 saw the launch of several new preparations, the result of a joint venture among Merck, Boehringer/Mannheim, and Knoll.

After World War I, Merck lost many of its foreign affiliates—among them Merck & Co. in the United States. In Germany, attention turned to vitamins as a new product category; Vigantol was introduced in 1927, followed by Cebion in 1934.

World War II was characterized by economic conditions similar to those of the earlier war, and the supply of skilled workers and raw materials grew smaller and smaller. By the end of the war, the greater part of the plant had been reduced to rubble; approximately 80 percent of the production capacity was destroyed.

American troops occupied the factory on March 25, 1945. Initially, the company was allowed only to remove debris and to salvage whatever usable machinery it could. On April 30, 1945, the military government granted the first production permit for drugs, and two months later the factory was also permitted to begin production of pesticides, food preservatives, and other chemicals for laboratory use.

A turning point came on June 20, 1948, with currency reform. Soon afterwards, the boom commonly known as the "Wirtschaftswunder," or economic miracle, set in, and the entire German economy began to rebound. For Merck, this turnaround brought double-digit sales growth for many years.

Successful pharmaceutical agents of this time included corticoid preparations (for example, Fortecortin, which is still used today), the cold remedy Nasivin, the hormone preparations Gestafortin and Menova, the antiallergy agent Ilvin, the sulfonamide Pallidin, the digestion stimulant Nutrizym, the broad-spectrum antibiotic Refobacin, and the cardiac agent Encordin.

In the chemical research sector, work started on pearl-lustre pigments in 1957, and on liquid crystals 10 years later. In the area of analytical chemistry, Merck played a leading role in the development of chromatographic methods.

In 1995, the legal form of Merck—until then managed as an oHG (open partnership)—was transformed into a KGaA (partnership limited by shares). The general partners, who together hold 74 percent of the capital stock, all belong to the Merck family circle.

Today, the Merck Group conducts its internationally oriented business in the three business sectors of pharmaceuticals, laboratory supplies, and specialty chemicals. There are 209 companies operating for Merck KGaA in 52 countries. They have production facilities in 60 locations in 26 countries.

The product range comprises more than 20,000 different items—drugs, vitamins, biomaterials, reagents, laboratory supplies, electronic chemicals, liquid crystals, and pigments—in addition to many related services.[1]

Sales Drivers:
Bone Healing and Resorbable Materials

With annual sales increases of 12 percent, reconstructive devices had once again led Biomet in sales. Although this increase was smaller than in years past, it was nevertheless a reflection of Biomet's strength in a market that had been shaken to its core by pricing pressure and competition.

In the summer of 1999, Piper Jaffray Senior Research Analyst Thomas Gunderson issued an industry report that declared, "The price concessions of the 1990s have subsided and the risk-reward equation is favorable again. With improving market dynamics, we continue to believe that selective investment in the orthopedics market will offer superior returns to the astute investor."[26]

In his report, which estimated the global orthopedics business at $10.5 billion, Gunderson made a number of predictions: industry consolidation would continue; niche markets, especially sports medicine implantables, would grow faster than the rest of the industry; and biologics would drive industry growth in the future.

In 1999, Lorenz Surgical received FDA clearance to market the Mimix Bone Substitute Material for craniofacial applications. Mimix was the first of Biomet's three planned resorbable bone substitutes for the domestic market; Lorenz Surgical was the ideal Biomet subsidiary to position Mimix for craniomaxillofacial clinicians.

Mimix is a calcium-based material mixed with a citric acid solution; it hardens to fill a void in bone, and it boasts an extremely slow resorption rate. It is usually used for the repair of neurosurgical burr holes, craniotomy cuts, and other cranial defects but can also be used in the restoration or augmentation of bony contours in a craniofacial procedure.[27]

According to Vice President of Biomaterials Technology Craig Blaschke, Mimix was part of Biomet's overall strategy of offering bone substitutes with a range of resorption rates so that doctors could select a product appropriate for a specific area.

"Our approach has been to employ a multiple material approach," he said. "We did not believe a single material with a single set of properties and resorption profile would satisfy all the different requirements in the body, and we believe our strategy will play out in the end."[28]

As their name implied, these bone substitutes could be used as bone fillers that the body would gradually absorb as real bone grew to replace them.

"Another biomaterials project under active development is the manufacture of orthopedic devices from polymers," Blaschke said. "These devices perform their function in the body—usually to mend a fracture or soft tissue injury—then dissolve after they have served that function.

"They are converted into water and carbon dioxide," he continued. "The implants are thermoplastic. They are never going to approach the strength of a titanium or stainless steel device, but through design considerations, changing the shape, for example, many metal plates can be replaced by resorbable thermoplastic."[29]

This strategy seemed to yield results fairly quickly. Joel Higgins, director of resorbable engineering, observed that Biomet quickly expanded its line of resorbable technologies beyond the plate and screw fixation devices marketed by Lorenz. "We branched out into arthroscopy indications with resorbable interference screws and resorbable staples," Higgins said.[30]

Bone and soft tissue fixation with polymer devices was born at Biomet through a joint venture with United States Surgical Corporation (U.S. Surgical). The cooperative effort was launched to develop, manufacture, and market bioresorbable implants. U.S. Surgical's experience in polymer technology brought the company success in the development of absorbable sutures and staples. Together the two companies produced pins and rods used in repairing broken bones. The venture made Biomet the

Vice President of Biomaterials Technology Craig Blaschke said Biomet's strategy in the developing bone substitute field brings both promise and challenge for the future of the company.

first company to apply resorbable technology to craniomaxillofacial applications. The LactoSorb family of products became an important asset, which was marketed through Lorenz Surgical.[31]

The 3i Acquisition

The most significant event of 1999 occurred on December 15, when Biomet announced the completion of the assimilation of Implant Innovations International (3i).[32] Biomet issued 11.7 million common shares for all of 3i's issued and outstanding shares.[33]

3i developed, manufactured, and marketed products for oral rehabilitation—dental reconstructive implants and related instrumentation, regenerative products and materials, and bone substitute materials.[34] Founded in 1987, 3i occupied an 80,000-square-foot headquarters and manufacturing facility in Palm Beach Gardens, Florida. The firm also had sales offices in Canada, Europe, and Mexico.[35]

Keith D. Beaty, 3i CEO, and Richard J. Lazzara, chairman, addressed the merger in a letter to 3i customers.

Since the orthopedic industry is also focused on implants that are placed in bone, we have much in common in the science, products and technologies we use and are developing. Biomet has many interesting products in development that could be very synergistic with our own needs. We believe some of these products may be instrumental in allowing 3i to apply leading edge technology for application in the dental field. In addition, some of the research activities and knowledge of implant surfaces at 3i may help Biomet to develop more competitive products in the orthopedic arena.

Beaty said 3i's interest in the merger also stemmed from the very similar management and culture of the two companies.

Biomet did things that were good for patients and improved products as opposed to always putting business first, which is a very strong philosophical requirement that we had. Financially and fiscally, Biomet was a very frugal team that didn't waste a lot of money and did things that made sense but at the same time . . . believed in letting a team of people work independently to be successful, as opposed to micromanaging.[36]

At the end of 1999, 3i was the second-largest manufacturer in the $250 million domestic market and the third-largest competitor in the

$740 million worldwide market for dental reconstructive implants. Its worldwide market share was approximately 16 percent.[37]

Dental reconstructive implants, developed more than 30 years ago, provided a natural appearance and could be a permanent replacement for missing teeth. A dental reconstructive implant consists of a small titanium screw or

Right: The synergistic merger between 3i and Biomet allowed 3i to expand its application in the dental field and Biomet to develop more competitive products in the orthopedic arena. From left are Niles Noblitt, 3i Chairman Richard Lazzara, 3i CEO Keith Beaty, and Dane Miller.

Below: Biomet acquired 3i, based in Palm Beach Gardens, Florida, in 1999. It is the second-largest manufacturer of dental reconstructive implants in the United States and the third-largest worldwide.

Left: 3i develops, manufactures, and markets products for oral rehabilitation—dental implants and related instrumentation, regenerative products and materials, and bone substitute materials.

Below: 3i's OSSEOTITE dental reconstructive implant system is its premier product. The system features a microporous surface for earlier attachment of the tooth to the implanted anchor and offers improved integration of bone and implant.

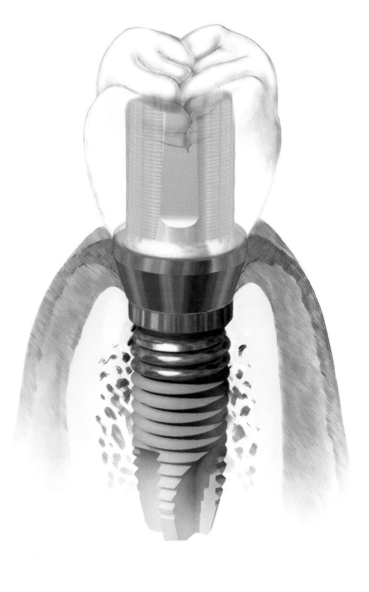

cylinder that is surgically implanted into the mandible or maxilla. The implant replaces the root of the missing tooth and provides an anchor for the new artificial tooth.[38]

According to the American Dental Association in 2000, there were approximately 5,000 periodontists, 6,200 oral surgeons, and 3,200 prosthodontists in the United States. Of these specialists, 95 percent of the oral surgeons, 75 percent of the periodontists, and 10 percent of the prosthodontists performed implant placement procedures. That resulted in a surgical specialist target market of nearly 10,000 clinicians.[39]

In the United States, Europe, and Japan, it was estimated that more than 200 million people had some degree of edentulism (one or more missing teeth) that could benefit from dental reconstructive implant therapy. With the estimated penetration of this market at only 4 to 8 percent, the room for growth was tremendous.[40]

3i Products

The OSSEOTITE dental implant system, which was 3i's premier product, featured a patented microporous surface that allowed for earlier loading (attaching the tooth to the implanted anchor) and offered better integration of bone to the surface of the implant than could competing dental implants. In 1998, the OSSEOTITE system received 510(k) clearance from the FDA to load after eight weeks of healing compared to the traditional 12 to 24 weeks associated with conventional dental implants.[41]

One of the latest products introduced by 3i had little to do with teeth. Its Platelet Concentrate Collection System (PCCS) was a custom-designed centrifuge system for the rapid preparation of autologous platelet concentrates. This compact system offered several notable advantages over more conventional products. The PCCS required a significantly smaller sample of blood, took up little space in office or ambulatory environments, and allowed for precise control of blood components.[42]

Another 1999 3i product, the ZiReal Post, was an all-ceramic abutment with a titanium interface incorporating the durability and strength of zirconia, the strongest ceramic compound available on the market. A key distinction of the ZiReal Post was its minimal risk of fracture, allowing the projection of light and color to approximate the translucency of natural teeth.[43]

With the acquisition of 3i at the end of 1999, Biomet's worldwide presence included six strategic business units operating 14 manufacturing facilities throughout the world. Altogether, the company employed more than 3,000 team members and more than 1,000 sales representatives.[44]

Biomet Orthopedics introduced 22 products in 2001, including (clockwise from top) the Ascent Revision Knee System, M^{2}a-Ringloc Acetabular Component, M^{2}a-Taper Metal-on-Metal Hip Articulation System, Repicci II Unicondylar Knee, and the Exact Hip Instrumentation System.

CHAPTER NINE

A VISION FOR THE FUTURE

2000 AND BEYOND

More important than my vision is the vision of everybody here. I think the most important aspects of leadership are creating an environment and then getting out of everybody's way so they can do their job.

—Dane A. Miller, Ph.D., president and CEO

AS THE MILLENNIUM DAWNED, Biomet stood on the brink of a great milestone: $1 billion in annual sales. For the longtime team members at Biomet, many of whom joined in the mid-1980s, when the company was doing nearly $30 million in sales, Biomet's growth seemed almost beyond belief. Yet the numbers were incontrovertible. For 23 consecutive years, Biomet had posted year-over-year revenue gains, oftentimes growing by double-digit percentages. In 2000, revenue increased another 11 percent to reach $920.6 million. It seemed almost certain that Biomet would cross the billion-dollar threshold within a year.[1]

"No quarter, from one year to the next, has ever been lower than the quarter the year before," said Lonnie Witham, senior regulatory specialist. "It's been a steady increase—just one line going up at a 45-degree angle. And as long as the current management is here, its philosophy is in place, and the great sales force that we have is in place, I don't see how that cannot continue."[2]

Yet CEO Dane Miller, who had predicted a billion in sales as far back as the acquisition of OEC, never measured the success of Biomet in purely financial terms. As he frequently remarked, the company's growth was due to the dedication of its team members, its superior products, its excellent relationship with the medical community, and the company's culture of improvement.

At least some of Biomet's success also had to do with its excellent timing. The company had entered an industry that was poised to explode. The aging of America, coupled with better implant materials and techniques, had resulted in a long market boom that swept through the entire orthopedic industry. Even during the pricing pressures of the 1990s, the orthopedic industry continued to grow. While most orthopedic companies benefited from this expansion, what distinguished Biomet was exactly how much it prospered. In general, the company outpaced its rivals, steadily expanding in both its geographic reach and its product offerings.

By 2000, Biomet was a solidly global company. Biomet International was a far-flung operation managed by Senior Vice President of International Operations Chuck Niemier, who oversaw direct operations in Europe, Canada, Puerto Rico, Mexico, Chile, Argentina, Korea, Japan, Australia, and New Zealand. Europe alone had 22 direct Biomet subsidiaries.

In both international and domestic markets, reconstructive devices continued to lead

The Bone Mulch Screw was a key Arthrotek implant product offered at the turn of the century.

the company in sales. In 2000, sales of hips, knees, and shoulders accounted for more than half of total sales.[3]

The Repicci

One of Biomet's advantages was the depth of its offerings. By the end of 2000, it occupied the number four spot in the U.S. reconstructive device market (then estimated to be $2.06 billion annually).[4] Biomet's broad range of products and technologies remained unmatched by any of its larger competitors. It offered the broadest range of total-hip products in the industry, with more than 20 systems addressing virtually every clinical need an orthopedic surgeon might encounter in the operating room.[5] In the total-knee market alone, Biomet offered nine major products in 2000.[6]

Like the company's other reconstructive products, the Repicci II Unicondylar Knee had been developed in conjunction with a surgeon and offered a distinct and unique advantage.

"The Repicci refers to the surgical technique of the small incision," said Dr. John Repicci, Biomet's partner. "The II refers to the stage of the osteoarthritis. In other words, once the patient has worn out the articular surface to the point where [there is] bone-on-bone contact in one part of the knee, it's stage II osteoarthritis. So the Repicci technique at stage II is how we [named] the prosthetic part."[7]

Using Repicci's technique and Biomet's knee, patients were able to undergo a knee implant and go home the same day with no pain.

The product was one that set Biomet apart, said Lance Perry, director of marketing in knee reconstruction.

Not only does it provide benefits for the surgeon who uses the product, it also provides a lot of benefits from a nontraditional orthopedic point of view. It specifically addresses rehabilitation issues—concerns about length of stay in the hospital, pain management—things that weren't traditionally thought about by orthopedic companies.[8]

Steady Sales

In addition to reconstructive devices, Biomet had strong sales in its many other businesses. The company's 3i subsidiary experienced a 30 percent increase in its worldwide sales of dental reconstructive implants, regenerative membranes, and bone substitute materials for reconstructive procedures of the jaw.[9]

Sales in the fixation category jumped 11 percent to $180.3 million. Biomet's VHS Vari-Angle Hip Fixation System continued to gain market share in the domestic market. Additionally, sales of EBI's Bone Healing System–Model 2001 increased better than 10 percent, while Lorenz Surgical's craniomaxillofacial products, including the newly released Mimix Bone Substitute, grew nearly 10 percent in sales.

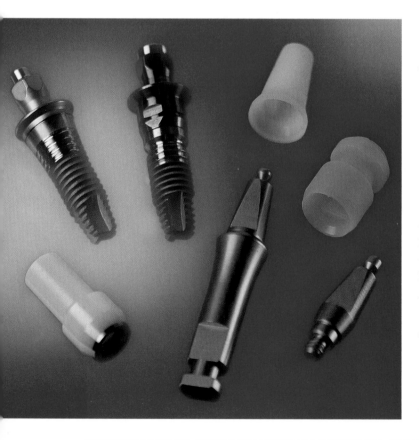

Biomet's 3i subsidiary launched seven new products in 2001, including Simple Logic Restorative components, the ZiReal Post, and the TG OSSEOTITE implant. Also pictured is the OSSEOTITE Dental Reconstructive implant.

At the end of the third quarter, EBI introduced the Dimension Wrist Fixator as well as the Access Pelvic Fixator. EBI's spinal product sales were led by a better than 50 percent leap in the spinal fixation trade in the United States.[10]

Biolectron

These steadily growing sales put the company in an excellent cash position, enabling it to continue its policy of smart acquisition. In late September 2000, EBI announced the acquisition of Allendale, New Jersey–based Biolectron for $90 million in cash.[11] Founded in 1977, Biolectron was a private company with annual sales of approximately $45 million. Its products addressed the spinal fusion, fracture healing, and arthroscopy market segments.[12]

"Biolectron competes effectively in the high-growth market segments where Biomet has an interest in expanding its product portfolio," Miller said at the time of the purchase. "We believe that this acquisition will be accretive to Biomet's earnings during fiscal year 2001 and beyond."[13]

Biolectron's noninvasive spinal stimulator, the SpinalPak System, complemented EBI's industry-leading implantable spinal fusion stimulation product. As a result of the increased product line, EBI was able to offer its customers spinal fusion stimulation technology for use in either inpatient or outpatient settings.[14]

"The attraction of Biolectron was really the noninvasive spinal fusion stimulation system

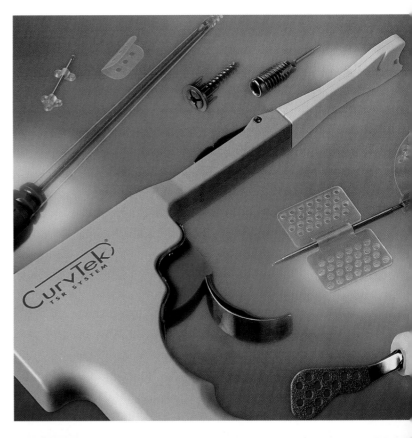

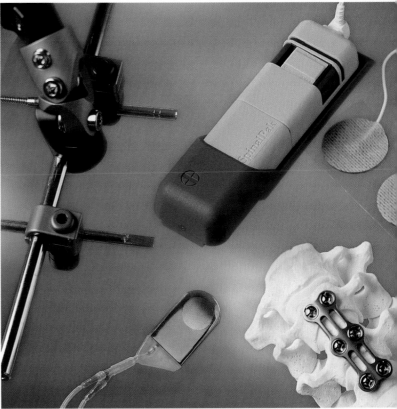

Top right: Lorenz Surgical introduced 14 new products in 2001, and Arthrotek launched nine. Clockwise from upper left are the LactoSorb Alveolar Distractor and Ethmoid Stent, LactoScrew Anchor with inserter, WasherLoc Tibial Graft Fixation device, Bone Mulch Screw, CurvTek Bone Tunneling System, LactoSorb Lefort III Distractor, and Total TMJ Replacement System.

Right: During 2001, EBI introduced 22 new products, including (clockwise from upper left) the OptiROM Elbow Fixator, SpinalPak Fusion Stimulation device, Vuelock Anterior Cervical Plate System, and OsteoGen-D 40/S Straight Cathode.

[SpinalPak]," said Greg Sasso, vice president of corporate development and communications. "It's been a great acquisition. The SpinalPak System continues to grow at very nice rates, and it was one of those kind of win/win situations. I think Dane and the principal owner of Biolectron negotiated a fair deal for both parties."[15]

Other Biolectron products included OrthoPak, a small, lightweight bone growth stimulation device approved by the FDA in 1986 for use in treating nonunion fractures, and the CurvTek Bone Tunneling System, a proprietary instrument for use in the reattachment of soft tissue to bone. This product, which received clearance from the FDA in October 1997, was merged into Arthrotek.[16]

Metal on Metal

Biomet's leadership position in high-technology articulation systems was reinforced in 2000 when the FDA gave it clearance to market the M^2a-Taper Metal-on-Metal Hip Articulation System,[17] designed to address younger, more active patients.[18] Biomet was the second company to receive FDA regulatory clearance for a metal-on-metal hip system.[19]

THE OXFORD MENISCAL KNEE

JUST ONE DAY AFTER AWAKING IN THE recovery room following his knee replacement surgery, 72-year-old Norman Crawford was walking. Two days later, he went home.

What made Crawford's quick recovery possible was a result of the Biomet-Merck joint venture—a reconstructive device called the Oxford Meniscal Knee.

Dr. James Rathbun, who performed Crawford's surgery in January 2001, was the first surgeon to use the Oxford medial unicompartmental arthroplasty procedure in its present form in North America. And even after performing the surgery more than a dozen times, he still finds the results remarkable.

"These patients have 100 degrees of knee flexion in the recovery room; they can straight leg raise and can flex the knee well past 100 degrees in the recovery room within 10 minutes. That's unheard of," said Rathbun, chief orthopedic surgeon at the Scarborough Hospital in Toronto, Canada.

"Certainly in the dozen procedures that I've done—and it is too early to give any long-term conclusions—it is remarkable to see how the patients can get up and out of bed and walk within two days and be home three days after surgery. That is remarkable, and we haven't seen that before," he said. "In many patients [with traditional total knee replacements], it takes weeks to get 90 degrees of knee flexion."

The Oxford Meniscal Knee replacement was developed with Biomet-Merck by Drs. John Goodfellow and John O'Connor at the Nuffield Orthopaedic Centre in Oxford, England, and was revised by Dr. David Murray. It is currently offered in hospitals around the world.

Designed specifically to address the issue of wear debris, the M²a-Taper Metal-on-Metal System offered patients and surgeons the most advanced system available. Validated by extensive testing, the new joint system combined the advantages of exceptionally low wear rates—.004mm a year, compared with .1mm to .2mm a year for conventional metal-on-polyethylene articulations—with the already proven superior performance of Biomet's acetabular and femoral components.[20]

The M²a-Taper was composed of a cobalt-chromium-molybdenum tapered insert that was set into a titanium acetabular shell.[21] One of the more striking characteristics associated with this all-metal joint system was its ability to repair itself. In-vitro wear testing showed that after the initial wear-in period, the articulation exhibited a "self-polishing" action that made the bearing surface smoother. Also, the body's natural synovial fluid lubricated the metal surfaces. As the patient's activities increased over time, it was believed that wear would likely decrease and scratches would not impair the articulation. Instead, over a period of time, scratches were actually removed by the polishing phenomenon.[22]

The metal-on-metal joint idea wasn't new. During the 1960s, first generation metal-on-metal devices showed great promise, but they experienced early failures that led to the abandonment of the idea.[23]

For example, component loosening was common in the first-generation devices. Further, there were concerns about the potential for carcinogenesis in people with these devices, resulting from increased metal ion levels.[24] Consequently, many surgeons abandoned them in favor of metal-on-polyethylene articulations, and the "forgiving" nature of polyethylene led to the wide acceptance of metal-on-polyethylene joints. However, increasing concerns about plastic debris and osteolysis (dissolution of the bone) led to the resurgence of metal-on-metal hip systems, and technological advancements have led to a second-generation metal-on-metal design that has solved the problems associated with the devices of the 1960s.[25]

"In a great number of patients, the wear and tear of the knee joint is limited to one side only, not both," said Rathbun. "So it makes sense to replace only the worn-out side." He noted that most of the time, the damage was in the medial compartment.

Based on Rathbun's preliminary results, not only did patients recover much more quickly; their hospital stays were cut in half. In addition, this novel procedure significantly reduced patients' pain levels and rehabilitation intensity and duration, compared with more traditional knee replacement procedures.

The Oxford knee arthroplasty required a limited incision—only two to three inches, compared with up to 12 inches for a traditional total replacement, and the distal femoral could be accomplished without dislocating the patella. The prosthesis was designed so the gliding polyethylene meniscal bearing remained fully congruent between the components of the prosthesis throughout the entire range of movement.

Rathbun said potential candidates for this procedure were usually 60 years old or older and suffered from osteoarthritis of the knee involving primarily a single compartment. Other critical indications included an intact anterior cruciate ligament, a passively correctable deformity, and a relatively normal lateral compartment. According to Rathbun, approximately one in four patients was eligible for this new partial knee replacement.

"I think before too long—if the benefits of this surgery prove to be as significant as I perceive from the first dozen I've done—this will be something that will be very commonly performed across the country by orthopedic surgeons," Rathbun concluded.[1]

Breaking the Billion Dollar Barrier

In summer 2000, Biomet predicted it would definitely cross the $1 billion line in revenue in the upcoming fiscal year. It also announced a $.16 per share cash dividend and a three-for-two stock split.[26]

"The declaration of this dividend and the three-for-two stock split is an expression of appreciation for the continued support of our shareholders as the company completes its first quarter with annualized sales exceeding $1 billion," Miller said.[27]

In 24 short years, the company had grown from a mere vision for an innovative orthopedic company to an established, major competitor in the worldwide musculoskeletal products market, with more than $1 billion in net sales and a market capitalization of approximately $9 billion.[28]

But Miller noted the trials that come with growth, saying, "Our biggest challenge as we pass through the $1 billion range and move toward $2 billion is to not start acting like we are a big company."

Miller said part of the reason Biomet grew ahead of the market was its ability to identify technical opportunities in the marketplace and technologies to address the problems.

We have created a new-product-and-technology flow that has been superior to most of our competitors'. We have been able to do that because our senior management, including myself, come from the ranks of science and engineering, which allows us to better understand technical needs and technologies to solve those needs.[29]

The company's prediction was right. In 2001, sales increased to $1.03 billion, Biomet's 24th record-setting year. Income rose to $197.5 million.[30]

Despite these impressive sales, the figures actually could have been higher. During fiscal year 2001, the company began establishing a direct sales operation in Japan to strengthen its position in the international marketplace. However, the reduction of product purchases from Biomet's former dealer organization in Japan

Below and left: More than 20 Biomet team members joined the Make-a-Wish Foundation to build this 55-by-10-foot fort for Kenny, whose cancer is in remission. Kenny is the son of Biomet PMI technician Dan Purkey. The 20-foot-high fort was one of the many projects Biomet team members participate in.

Only one available cemented hip in the world can claim proven clinical success for over 35 years: Biomet Orthopedics' Stanmore Modular Hip System. Developed by Biomet's OEC operations in Europe, the product retains its original geometry, surface finish, and material.

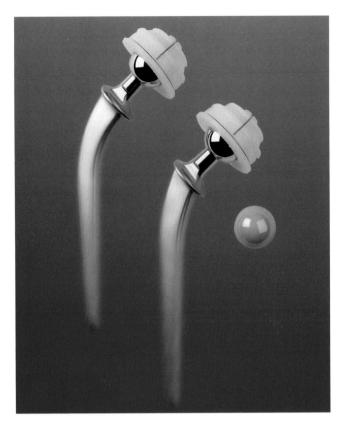

resulted in a drop of approximately $6 million in revenue during the year.[31]

A Living Collaboration

In August 2001, Biomet announced an agreement with Organogenesis, the first tissue engineering company to gain FDA marketing approval for a mass-produced product containing living cells. The agreement granted Biomet the right to globally develop and commercialize orthopedic and periodontal products comprising the Organogenesis FortaFlex bioengineered matrix technology.

While both parties would be responsible for product development, Biomet would provide the

BONE-DEEP VALUE

BIOMET CEO DANE MILLER IS NO LARRY Bird. He said it himself. If he were, he could justify a multimillion-dollar salary. But until that day, he'll stick to his comparatively modest, no-stock-options pay. He blasts companies that pay CEOs exorbitant salaries.

"At some point you're just satisfying an uncontrollable greed complex," Miller told *Business Week* in 1992. He made a repeat appearance in the magazine's annual pay-for-performance analysis for his then $135,000-a-year average pay from 1989 to 1991. This was a time when other CEOs were taking home millions. Biomet shareholders scored a staggering 661 percent return for those three years.[1]

Miller said he believes the best way to compensate an executive is through equity, the reward of success he can reap just as his shareholders do.[2]

"In professional sports, you're buying the entity," Miller explained. "People buy Celtics tickets because they want to see Larry Bird, but no one buys a Coke because of its CEO."

As Miller told the *Washington Times* in 1991, "How could I justify taking home a seven-digit salary when there are people in training positions in our company making $6 an hour?"

In 2000, Miller still led the list in terms of shareholder value relative to his salary, fellow founder Jerry Ferguson said. "He's one of the lowest-paid CEOs for a company of this size in the country," Ferguson said.[3]

Even in 2000, no annual salary for any top Biomet official surpassed $393,000 a year;[4] and neither Miller nor Noblitt is the highest paid team member of the company.

funding. Dr. Michael Sabolinski, president and CEO of Organogenesis, praised the partnership in a press release.

Organogenesis is a leader in tissue engineering; Biomet is a leader in orthopedic products. We believe the combination of our FortaFlex technology and Biomet's product development expertise could yield a number of products for the orthopedic and periodontal markets.[32]

Digital Surgery

Biomet tapped into image-guided software when it announced a strategic alliance with z-kat, of Hollywood, Florida, in February 2002. The venture drew on the vast potential for the integration of computing technology with the implantation of medical devices. Z-kat and Biomet would codevelop and distribute image-guided surgical applications in all of Biomet's business fields.[33]

Z-kat developed intelligent instrumentation and human-interactive robotic technologies for minimally invasive musculoskeletal and neurological surgeries. Biomet would put this expertise to use in each of its business fields, including orthopedic reconstruction, fixation, spinal, arthroscopic, maxillofacial, and dental surgeries.[34]

A Growing Market

The reconstructive device market for total hip and knee procedures was estimated to grow at 10 to 13 percent per year. This strength had several causes. Among them was the increased willingness of orthopedic surgeons to provide a variety of treatment options for their younger patients. In addition, the number of suitable elderly patients was climbing as a result of new products and technologies and improved instrumentation.[35]

Additionally, elderly individuals were healthier, due to improved lifestyles and better medical care. As the elderly population worldwide continued to

This NASDAQ television advertisement brought additional national attention to Biomet in 2001.

grow, Biomet was well positioned to grow commensurately.[36] Miller explained how that potential growth could rival, if not surpass, what Biomet had already experienced.

The 75-and-older population is living longer, healthier lives. To a great extent, I believe it's because of medical technology. Today's 85-year-old patient is probably as healthy as the 75-year-old patient was 25 years ago.

Keep in mind that when you replace a hip or a knee, the patient is remobilized. The things that would slow them down later in life, such as congestive heart failure and pulmonary problems, don't do so because they can be active again.

We're looking at a larger population, and we're looking at that 55-plus population growing dramatically in the next 10 or 20 years. We think when you combine all those factors with the need, in some cases, to revise implants 10, 15, 20 years [later], our market for total joint replacement could double in the next 10 to 15 years.[37]

Biologic Solutions versus Orthopedics

As biotechnology companies discover formulas to combat degenerative diseases such as arthritis, the role of prosthetics is expected to diminish. But Biomet Director of Biomaterials Engineering Robert Ronk said hardware will not be completely replaced.

"Biologics, I think, is definitely going to take over orthopedics at some point," Ronk said. "Whether that's in five years or 15 years or 25 years, I don't know. But the ability to take cells or genes and allow the body to heal itself, so to speak, I think is definitely going to happen. There will be biologic solutions to the degenerative diseases that really affect a lot of people."[38]

But while the technology in some areas of medicine is replacing the surgeon, such as in cardiology, orthopedic surgeon John Cuckler said the technology of arthritis has decades ahead of it before the prosthetic replacement of joints becomes antiquated.[39]

Above: Margie Morrow was diagnosed with severe rheumatoid arthritis at 17. By the age of 36, she was confined to a wheelchair, where she sat for 11 years. After a series of joint replacement surgeries using Biomet products, Margie was walking on her own two feet.

Opposite: Biomet's corporate headquarters and largest manufacturing facility are still located in Warsaw, Indiana.

RECESSION RESISTANT

THOUGH THREE RECESSIONS HAVE hit the United States since Biomet was founded, the company's hometown of Warsaw, Indiana, has hardly suffered. Even in 2001, after the combined effects of a national recession and the September 11 terrorist attacks cost more than one million Americans their jobs in three months, Warsaw retailers continued to ring in steady sales, builders erected new structures, and "help wanted" signs hung in many store windows.

Warsaw's 13,000 people owed their consistently low unemployment rate to the fact that they shared the community with three of the five top orthopedic companies, which together had nearly a third of the $13 billion global market.

Warsaw is the undisputed capital of the orthopedic industry and has been since 1895, when DePuy was founded. A DePuy salesman started Zimmer in 1915. A former Zimmer salesman started Orthopedic Equipment Company (later acquired by Biomet), and former Zimmer employees Dane Miller and Jerry Ferguson, along with former OEC employees Niles Noblitt and Ray Harroff, formed Biomet in 1977. Together, these orthopedic giants employed one quarter of Warsaw residents in 2001. All three plan to expand and add skilled workers in coming years.[1]

"So I think that the clinician and the company are in very safe territory in regard to demand for their products and services," he added. Market conditions and regulatory restrictions led Cuckler to believe there will be no major leaps forward in the near future. "I think we'll continue to see an evolution in the Darwinian sense—not always recognizable as progress, but you look back some years later and you say, 'Gee, that was an important step out of the primordial climb to where we are today.'"[40]

Garry England, senior vice president of Warsaw operations, agreed that biomaterials to replace bone or metals and plastic are on the horizon.

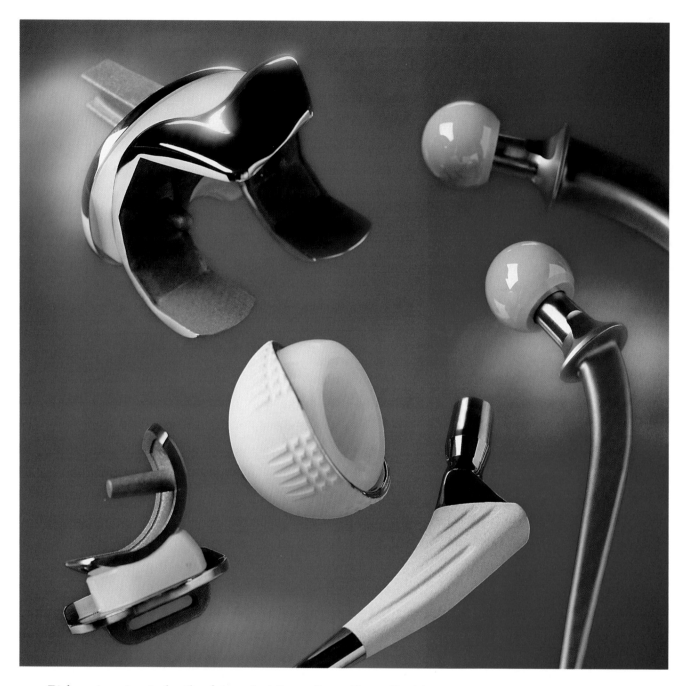

Biology is going to be the future, but it won't obsolete what we're doing. There's always going to be a need for structural engineering of artificial joints. Orthopedics has been a field that evolves. You don't see revolutionary changes, but you see improvements every year, and you build on what you learned in the past.

One of the key reasons is you don't know if what you're doing is successful until 15 years later, because it's not like a drug, which either

Biomet-Merck introduced 20 products in 2001, including (clockwise from top right) two Stanmore Long Hip Stems, the Aura II Hip Stem, the Advantage Hip Cup, the Oxford Unicompartmental Knee, and the Oxford Total Meniscal Knee.

works quickly or it doesn't. Things that appear to work after they've been implanted for one or two years may have a high failure rate at five years

THE BEST THING SINCE SLICED BREAD

NAME BRAND LOYALTY IS COMMON when it comes to shoes and purses. But for one man it applies to body parts.

Ted Dobbins has been in the Buildings and Grounds Maintenance Department for more than a decade. The physical work became difficult in the mid-1990s, when he began having knee problems.

"I was limping. Couldn't hardly get around," he said. "They hurt from the time I [got up] in the morning until the time I put them in bed at night. I was in pain 24 hours a day."[1]

Doctors told Dobbins he was too young to have his knees replaced and put him on medication. Finally, in January of 2001, he decided he could wait no more.

"They wanted to try another medicine, and I said, 'No. I've had enough,'" Dobbins recalled. "I said, 'I want you to do the operation, and I want Biomet knees.'"[2]

On February 13, 2001, he had bilateral knee surgery. The next day his feet gingerly hit the floor, and he began walking on Biomet AGC knees—with a little help from a walker. Four months later, he was back to work full time.

"It's the best decision I ever made," Dobbins boasted. "Right now I have no pain at all, and I really can't tell the difference between my knees ten years ago and what I have now. It's the best thing since sliced bread."[3]

Chairman of the Board Niles Noblitt, seated, and President and CEO Dane Miller, Ph.D., two of the four founders, led the Biomet team into the 21st century and the company's 25th successful year of operations.

or 10 years. We have some products now that have had good clinical results for 15 to 17 years. So you've got to be real careful, when you change something, that you don't do more harm than good.[41]

Changes in the orthopedic field were often referred to as evolutionary, rather than revolutionary; after all, Biomet was not trying to reinvent the wheel.

"I think for a while we've been making small, detailed steps improving the implants we have," said Troy Hershberger, director of product development for hips and knees. "And while a lot of people see that as technology stagnating, it really isn't, because the details are what make things last or [not] last. The devil is in the details."[42]

In fact, technology at Biomet was far from stagnant. "The biggest challenge now is just deciding which technology to put the resources behind," said Joel Higgins, director of resorbable engineering. "That's an almost daunting task at this point because there is just so much available out there, and the question becomes which is going to be the most advantageous from a market and a patient standpoint."[43]

The Road Ahead

There is no telling what orthopedic advances await, considering the advancements in the last 25 years. At the time Biomet was founded, a patient undergoing total hip replacement would stay in the hospital for two weeks. In 2001, it was about four days.[44] Similarly, it used to require several weeks to manufacture an artificial hip. By 2001, that time had been reduced to a few days.

John Susaraba, director of marketing for Biomet hips, attributed his faith in the company's future to its strong base of engineering expertise.

"If you look at the senior management of Biomet, more of them will have engineering degrees than business degrees, and that means that we will always be looking at new technologies that will benefit the market and help us continue to grow," said Susaraba. "So I think the future is very, very bright."[45]

Doctors in the field would continue to rely upon Biomet—not only for innovative products but for responsive service, said surgeon John Cuckler.

The team spirit is probably the highest in the industry. I think the product line reflects the sophistication of the management staff in terms of selecting the technology that is both clinically effective and cost effective. I think Dane Miller gets a large part of the credit for having quite a sophisticated and high level of insight into biomaterials and the people that he attracted around him, who are equally skilled and experienced. It's made for a business environment that is responsive and makes the right decision at the right time.

The designs that have been used were largely the result of collaboration between the engineering and management staff of Biomet and top-flight clinicians who brought their insight and married it to the technical and manufacturing sophistication of the company, which is what has produced a very successful business venture.[46]

Analysts agree that doctors don't switch suppliers easily. Sales are largely based upon the relationships sales reps build with physicians, said Andrew Jay, analyst with First Union Securities. "A good rep can really help. One of the key differentiators is the relationship between the sales force and the physician. Biomet has those relationships."[47]

Biomet's broad product offerings, strong intellectual property position, with over 750 issued and pending patents, and growing sales forces should allow the company to achieve its goals.

At Biomet, team members have the best of both worlds, said Dan Williamson, who came to the company in 1990 and serves as director of business development.

"We're in it for the good of humanity, for ourselves, for our parents, for our grandparents, cousins, and friends, but at the same time, it's our job, it's our career," Williamson said. "So we try to be visionaries, try to be innovative, and go out there and do good things for people, develop solutions for orthopedic problems. That's what we do, because, don't forget, we could all be patients someday."[48]

NOTES TO SOURCES

Chapter One

1. "Dane Alan Miller, Ph.D. Resume," n.d., Biomet archive.
2. Ibid.
3. "Jerry L. Ferguson Resume," n.d., Biomet archive.
4. Dane Miller resume.
5. Jerry Ferguson resume.
6. "Biomet . . . The Early Years," internal document, Biomet archive, 23 February 2000, 1.
7. "Niles L. Noblitt Resume," n.d., Biomet archive; "Ray Harroff Resume," n.d., Biomet archive.
8. Ray Harroff, interviewed by Richard F. Hubbard, tape recording, 2 April 2001, Write Stuff Enterprises.
9. Tom Mallory, M.D., interviewed by Richard F. Hubbard, tape recording, 8 November 2001, Write Stuff Enterprises.
10. Mary Louise Miller, interviewed by Richard F. Hubbard, tape recording, 13 March 2002, Write Stuff Enterprises.
11. Nancy Noblitt, interviewed by Richard F. Hubbard, tape recording, 12 March 2002, Write Stuff Enterprises.
12. Securities and Exchange Commission Form 10-K, Fiscal year ended 31 May 2000, Biomet.
13. Ibid.
14. David Cassak, "Biomet's Contrarian Conservatism," *In Vivo*, May 1999, 48–49.
15. Ibid.
16. Jeff Kurowski, "Indiana Business's Industrialist of the Year; Dane Miller, CEO of Biomet," *Indiana Business*, December 1989, 8.
17. Mark Vandewalle, interviewed by Jeffrey L. Rodengen, tape recording, 17 May 2001, Write Stuff Enterprises.
18. John O'Hanlon, "Musculoskeletal Medical," WSCR.COM, 25 September–1 October 2000, 25.
19. Cassak, "Biomet's Contrarian Conservatism," 48–49.
20. Dave Montgomery, interviewed by Richard F. Hubbard, tape recording, 17 May 2001, Write Stuff Enterprises.
21. "Biomet . . . The Early Years," 1.
22. Kurowski, "Industrialist of the Year," 8.
23. Norma Ferguson, interviewed by Richard F. Hubbard, tape recording, 19 March

2002, Write Stuff Enterprises.

24. Mary Louise Miller, interview.

25. Nancy Noblitt, interview.

26. Information provided by Niles Noblitt to Heather Deeley, April 2002.

27. Miles Igo, interviewed by Richard F. Hubbard, tape recording, 14 November 2001, Write Stuff Enterprises.

28. Ibid.

29. Ray Harroff, interview.

30. Ibid.

31. Kurowski, "Industrialist of the Year," 8.

32. Jerry Ferguson, interviewed by Richard F. Hubbard, tape recording, 18 May 2001, Write Stuff Enterprises.

33. Ibid.

34. Ibid.

35. Nancy Noblitt, interview.

36. Ray Harroff, interview.

37. Jerry Ferguson, interview.

38. Charles Niemier, interviewed by Richard F. Hubbard, tape recording, 30 August 2001, Write Stuff Enterprises.

39. Ibid.

40. Merrill Ritter, M.D., interviewed by Richard F. Hubbard, tape recording, 9 November 2001, Write Stuff Enterprises.

41. Ray Harroff, interview.

42. Niemier, interview.

43. Norma Ferguson, interview.

44. Nancy Noblitt, interview.

45. Ibid.

46. Information provided by Niles Noblitt.

47. Jerry Ferguson, interview.

48. Kurowski, "Industrialist of the Year," 8.

49. Dan Cordill, interviewed by Richard F. Hubbard, tape recording, 30 August 2001, Write Stuff Enterprises.

50. Ibid.

51. Ray Harroff, interview.

52. Cassak, "Biomet's Contrarian Conservatism," 49.

53. Information provided by Niles Noblitt.

54. Brian Howey, "Biomet: Bringing R&D to Market," *Indiana Business*, May 1988, 72.

55. Biomet 1997 Annual Report, 2.

56. Garry England, interviewed by Richard F. Hubbard, tape recording, 17 May 2001, Write Stuff Enterprises.

57. Cassak, "Biomet's Contrarian Conservatism," 49.

58. Jerry Ferguson, interview.

59. Cassak, "Biomet's Contrarian Conservatism," 49.

60. Dane Miller, interviewed by Jeffrey L. Rodengen, tape recording, 17 May 2001, Write Stuff Enterprises.

61. Biomet 1981 Annual Report, 5; Michael M. Harshbarger, Investment Research Industry Report: Orthopedic Devices, The Chicago Corporation, 24 October 1984, 6.

62. Dane Miller, interview.

63. Information provided by Niles Noblitt.

64. Biomet 1997 Annual Report, 2.

65. Ibid., 3.

66. "Biomet . . . The Early Years," 1.

67. Dane Miller, interview.

68. Mary Louise Miller, interview.

69. Kurowski, "Industrialist of the Year," 8.

70. Jerry Miller, interviewed by Richard F. Hubbard, tape recording, 16 October 2001, Write Stuff Enterprises.

71. Ray Harroff, interview.

72. Jerry Ferguson, interview.

73. Biomet 1997 Annual Report, 3.

74. Jerry Miller, interview.

75. Kenneth Miller, interviewed by Richard F. Hubbard, tape recording, 17 October 2001, Write Stuff Enterprises.

76. Biomet 1997 Annual Report, 3.

77. "Biomet, Inc.," internal document, Biomet archive, 1980.
78. "Biomet Breaks Ground For Building," *Times-Union,* 1 April 1980, 19.
79. "Biomet . . . The Early Years," 2.
80. Biomet 1997 Annual Report, 21.
81. Cassak, "Biomet's Contrarian Conservatism," 49.
82. Ibid.
83. Ibid., 49–50.
84. Tim Weis, interviewed by Richard F. Hubbard, tape recording, 15 November 2001, Write Stuff Enterprises.
85. Ibid.
86. Dane Miller, interview.
87. Ray Harroff, interview.
88. Cassak, "Biomet's Contrarian Conservatism," 50.
89. Ibid.
90. Biomet 1981 Annual Report, 8.
91. Biomet 1982 Annual Report, 4.
92. Biomet 1981 Annual Report, 5.
93. Ibid.
94. Ibid., 6.
95. Ibid.
96. Ibid., 8.
97. Ibid.

**Chapter One Sidebar:
The History of Orthopedics**

1. http://www. worldortho.com/ history1.html, 2001.
2. http://www.amirmd. com//ortho-info/ Ortho-history.html, 2001.
3. Ibid.
4. http://www. orthopaedic.com/ pehip.htm, 2001.
5. Ibid.
6. http://www.niams. nih.gov/hi/topics/ hip.htm, 2001.
7. Ibid.
8. http://bolandpc.ces. clemson.edu/ biomaterials/project1. htm, 2001.
9. http://www. medhelpnet.com/ medhist8.html, 2001.
10. http://bolandpc.ces. clemson.edu/ biomaterials/project1. htm, 2001.
11. http://kneesandhips. com/hip/charnley. htm, 2001.
12. http://www.nih.gov/ niams/healthinfo/ hiprepqa.htm, 2001.

**Chapter One Sidebar:
Keeping It in the Family**

1. Dane Miller, interview.
2. Ibid.
3. Ibid.
4. "Biomet . . . The Early Years," 2.
5. Dane Miller, interview.
6. "Biomet . . . The Early Years," 2.
7. Ibid.
8. Ibid.
9. Ibid.
10. Ray Harroff, interview.

Chapter Two

1. Jerry Ferguson, interview.
2. Dane Miller, interview.
3. Gina Smalley, "Biomet: Small Firm Becomes Local Success Story," *Times-Union,* 25 January 1983, Sec. II.
4. Ibid.
5. Cassak, "Biomet's Contrarian Conservatism," 50.
6. Berkley Duck, interviewed by Richard F. Hubbard, tape recording, 19 November 2001, Write Stuff Enterprises.
7. Information provided by Dane Miller to Heather Deeley, April 2002.
8. Biomet 1982 Annual Report, 2.
9. Norma Ferguson, interview.
10. Ibid.
11. Ibid.
12. Mary Louise Miller, interview.
13. Biomet 1982 Annual Report, 16.
14. Lee Ritchey, interviewed by Richard F. Hubbard, tape recording, 7 March 2002, Write Stuff Enterprises.
15. Biomet 1982 Annual Report, 2.
16. Ibid.
17. Ibid.
18. Mallory, interview.
19. Ritter, interview.
20. John McDaniel, interviewed by Richard F. Hubbard, tape recording, 15 November 2001, Write Stuff Enterprises.
21. Securities and Exchange Commission Form, 31 May 2000.

22. Kurowski, "Industrialist of the Year," 8.
23. Biomet 1997 Annual Report, 9.
24. Securities and Exchange Commission Form, 31 May 2000.
25. Tony Fleming, interviewed by Richard F. Hubbard, tape recording, 17 May 2001, Write Stuff Enterprises.
26. Biomet 1983 Annual Report, 4.
27. Ibid., 24.
28. Biomet 1997 Annual Report, 7.
29. Biomet 1983 Annual Report, 3.
30. Ibid., 7.
31. Biomet 1984 Annual Report, 17.
32. Cassak, "Biomet's Contrarian Conservatism," 51.
33. Ibid., 50.
34. Ibid., 51.
35. Dane Miller, interview.
36. Ibid.
37. Delmas Stiles, interviewed by Richard F. Hubbard, tape recording, 28 March 2002, Write Stuff Enterprises.
38. Ibid.
39. Bob Border, interviewed by Richard F. Hubbard, tape recording, 2 November 2001, Write Stuff Enterprises.
40. Ibid.
41. Niemier, interview.
42. Cheryl McIntosh, interviewed by Richard F. Hubbard, tape recording, 28 March 2002, Write Stuff Enterprises.
43. Stiles, interview.
44. Jack Wilhite, interviewed by Richard F. Hubbard, 28 March 2001, Write Stuff Enterprises.
45. Biomet 1984 Annual Report, 6.
46. John Deming, interviewed by Richard F. Hubbard, tape recording, 15 November 2001, Write Stuff Enterprises.
47. Ibid.
48. Biomet 1985 Annual Report, 6.
49. Information provided by Dane Miller.
50. Biomet 1985 Annual Report, 6.
51. Ibid.
52. Ibid., 23.
53. *Orange County Business Journal,* 17 March 1986, Vol. 9, No. 5.
54. Tom Allen, interviewed by Richard F. Hubbard, tape recording, 29 August 2001, Write Stuff Enterprises.
55. Ibid.
56. Ibid.
57. Biomet 1986 Annual Report, 4.
58. Ibid.
59. Ibid., 8.
60. Ibid.
61. Ibid., 4.
62. "New Implants Help Joints 'Get Moving,' " *Network,* May–June 1988, 3.
63. Mary Louise Miller, interview.
64. Biomet 1986 Annual Report, 12.
65. Ibid.
66. Ibid.
67. Ibid., 4.
68. Ibid., 19.
69. Ibid., 12.
70. Norma Ferguson, interview.
71. Mary Louise Miller, interview.
72. Barb Akers, interviewed by Richard F. Hubbard, tape recording, 1 November 2001, Write Stuff Enterprises.
73. Darlene Whaley, interviewed by Jeffrey L. Rodengen, tape recording, 17 May 2001, Write Stuff Enterprises.

Chapter Two Sidebar: The Wings of Biomet

1. Allen, interview.
2. Greg Garber, interviewed by Richard F. Hubbard, tape recording, 28 August 2001, Write Stuff Enterprises.
3. Ibid.
4. Ibid.
5. Ibid.
6. Ibid.
7. Ibid.
8. Ibid.
9. Ibid.
10. Ibid.
11. Ibid.

Chapter Three

1. Biomet 1987 Annual Report, 27.

2. Ibid., 11.
3. Ibid., 18.
4. Ibid.
5. Fleming, interview.
6. Biomet 1988 Annual Report, 2.
7. Ibid., 34.
8. Ibid., 13.
9. "The Business and Medicine Report," *In Vivo.*
10. James Pastena, interviewed by Richard F. Hubbard, tape recording, 11 March 2002, Write Stuff Enterprises.
11. Niemier, interview.
12. Ibid.
13. Daniel Hann, interviewed by Richard F. Hubbard, tape recording, 18 May 2001, Write Stuff Enterprises.
14. Biomet 1988 Annual Report, 2.
15. Ibid., 34.
16. Ibid., 3.
17. http://www.ebimedical.com, 2001.
18. Biomet 1988 Annual Report, 2.
19. http://www.ebimedical.com, 2001.
20. Cassak, "Biomet's Contrarian Conservatism," 51.
21. Ibid.
22. Ibid.
23. Ibid.
24. Ibid.
25. Dane Miller, interview.
26. Nancy Noblitt, interview.
27. John Wagoner, interviewed by Jeffrey L. Rodengen, tape recording, 17 May 2001, Write Stuff Enterprises.
28. Biomet 1987 Annual Report, 3.
29. Biomet 1988 Annual Report, 13.
30. Biomet 1987 Annual Report, 3.
31. Ibid.
32. Ibid.
33. Biomet 1988 Annual Report, 8.
34. Biomet 1987 Annual Report, 3.
35. Biomet 1988 Annual Report, 11.
36. Ibid., 13.
37. "The Corporate Elite," *Business Week,* 21 October 1988, 108.
38. Biomet 1988 Annual Report, 11.
39. Biomet 1989 Annual Report, 22–23.
40. Ibid., 23.
41. Ibid., 10.
42. http://www.aaos.org, 2002.
43. Biomet 1989 Annual Report, 21.
44. Ibid., 6.
45. Ibid., 7.
46. Ibid., 25.
47. *European Trade Report,* December 1989, 1.
48. Allen, interview.
49. Biomet 1989 Annual Report, 3.

Chapter Three Sidebar: An Imperfect Science

1. Dane Miller, interview.
2. David Brown, interviewed by Richard F. Hubbard, tape recording, 2 November 2001, Write Stuff Enterprises.
3. Ibid.
4. Whaley, interview.
5. Dean Golden, interviewed by Richard F. Hubbard, tape recording, 29 August 2001, Write Stuff Enterprises.
6. Jim Haller, interviewed by Richard F. Hubbard, tape recording, 18 May 2001, Write Stuff Enterprises.
7. Whaley, interview.
8. Ibid.
9. Wagoner, interview.
10. Ibid.

Chapter Four

1. Biomet 1990 Annual Report, 1.
2. Ibid., 17.
3. Ibid.
4. http://kneesandhips.com/hip/hipdise.htm, 2001.
5. Ibid.
6. Ibid.
7. Biomet 1990 Annual Report, 17.
8. Ibid.
9. Ibid., 7.
10. Ibid.
11. Ibid.
12. Ibid., 25.
13. http://www.ebimedical.com, 2001.
14. Biomet 1990 Annual Report, 7.
15. Ibid., 3.
16. Biomet 1991 Annual Report, 38.
17. Ibid., 42.
18. Jim Babcock, interviewed by

Richard F. Hubbard, tape recording, 30 August 2001, Write Stuff Enterprises.
19. Ibid.
20. Biomet 1991 Annual Report, 2.
21. Biomet 1997 Annual Report, 15.
22. *Bio Briefs*, spring 1991, 2; "Biomet 1997 Annual Report, 15.
23. Biomet 1991 Annual Report, 8.
24. Ibid., 12.
25. Ibid.
26. Ibid., 6.
27. Ibid., 7.
28. Henry Ames Finn, M.D., interviewed by Richard F. Hubbard, tape recording, 16 November 2001, Write Stuff Enterprises.
29. Ibid.
30. Ibid.
31. Dane Miller, *CEO Interviews*, 26 August 1991, 5924.
32. Ibid.
33. *Bio Briefs*, spring 1991, 1.
34. Biomet 1991 Annual Report, 22.
35. Ibid.
36. Ibid., 16.
37. John White, interviewed by Richard F. Hubbard, tape recording, 30 August 2001, Write Stuff Enterprises.
38. Babcock, interview.
39. White, interview.
40. Ibid.
41. Bill Kolter, interviewed by Jeffrey L. Rodengen, tape recording, 18 May

2001, Write Stuff Enterprises.
42. Troy Hershberger, interviewed by Richard F. Hubbard, tape recording, 17 May 2001, Write Stuff Enterprises.
43. Ibid.
44. Cordill, interview.
45. White, interview.
46. Biomet 1991 Annual Report, 42.
47. Ibid.
48. Biomet 1991 Annual Report, 13; http://www.wales.gov.uk/assemblydata, 2001.
49. Biomet 1991 Annual Report, 13.

**Chapter Four Sidebar:
A Knight in Shining Armor**

1. White, interview.

Chapter Five

1. Biomet 1992 Annual Report, 3.
2. Hershberger, interview.
3. David Smith, "Biomet chief shares success secret," *Journal and Courier*.
4. Biomet 1992 Annual Report, 6.
5. Jerry Ferguson, interview.
6. Steve Stewart, interviewed by Richard F. Hubbard, tape recording, 17 May 2001, Write Stuff Enterprises.
7. Ibid.
8. Don Boggs, interviewed by Richard F.

Hubbard, tape recording, 16 November 2001, Write Stuff Enterprises.
9. Greg Sasso, interviewed by Richard F. Hubbard, tape recording, 17 May 2001, Write Stuff Enterprises.
10. Sam Stutzman, interviewed by Jeffrey L. Rodengen, tape recording, 17 May 2001, Write Stuff Enterprises.
11. Golden, interview.
12. Ibid.
13. Greg Hartman, interviewed by Jeffrey L. Rodengen, tape recording, 17 May 2001, Write Stuff Enterprises.
14. Vandewalle, interview.
15. Richard Borror, interviewed by Richard F. Hubbard, tape recording, 17 May 2001, Write Stuff Enterprises.
16. Christine Shenot, "Biomet's Dane Miller: Team focus seeks to stifle bureaucracy, not initiative," *Investor's Business Daily*, 4 February 1992.
17. Biomet 1992 Annual Report, 6.
18. Ibid.
19. Cordill, interview.
20. Biomet 1992 Annual Report, 3.
21. Ibid., 5.
22. *Bio Briefs*, spring 1992, 1.
23. Ibid.

24. William Head, M.D., interviewed by Richard F. Hubbard, tape recording, 19 November 2001, Write Stuff Enterprises.
25. *Bio Briefs*, spring 1992, 1.
26. Kevin Stone, interviewed by Richard F. Hubbard, tape recording, 29 August 2001, Write Stuff Enterprises.
27. Biomet 1992 Annual Report, 17.
28. *Bio Briefs*, spring 1992, 4.
29. Ibid.
30. Biomet 1992 Annual Report, 9.
31. "Biomet Plans to Buy Lorenz Surgical," *South Bend Tribune*, 26 April 1992.
32. *Bio Briefs*, summer 1992, 1.
33. Ibid.; *Bio Briefs*, spring 1993, 1.
34. Hann, interview.
35. Jerry Ferguson, interview.
36. Joel Pratt, interviewed by Jeffrey L. Rodengen, tape recording, 18 May 2001, Write Stuff Enterprises.
37. *Bio Briefs*, summer 1993, 1.
38. Biomet 1992 Annual Report, 25.
39. *Bio Briefs*, winter 1993, 1.
40. Biomet 1993 Annual Report, 10.
41. Ibid., 5.
42. *Bio Briefs*, winter 1993, 2.

43. Biomet 1993 Annual Report, 2.
44. Biomet 1994 Annual Report, 10.
45. *Bio Briefs*, spring 1993, 3.
46. Biomet 1993 Annual Report, 2.
47. Ibid., 3.
48. Hershberger, interview.
49. *Bio Briefs*, fall 1992, 2.
50. Ibid.
51. Adolph Lombardi, M.D., interviewed by Richard F. Hubbard, tape recording, 17 November 2001, Write Stuff Enterprises.
52. Biomet 1994 Annual Report, 4.
53. *Bio Briefs*, summer 1993, 1.
54. Dan Spalding, "Biomet Exec Decries Regulatory Restraints," *Times-Union*, 2 March 1993.

Chapter Five Sidebar: Lending a Hand

1. *Bio Briefs*, summer 1997, 1.

Chapter Six

1. Cassak, "Biomet's Contrarian Conservatism," 53.
2. Ibid.
3. Ibid.
4. Ibid.
5. Biomet 1994 Annual Report, 8.
6. Department of Commerce, *Statistical Abstract of the United States: 1993*, 113th edition (Washington, D.C., 1993).
7. Biomet 1994 Annual Report, 2.
8. Lisa Kempfer, "CAD: Just what the doctor ordered," *Computer-aided Engineering*, September 1995, 34–43.
9. Cassak, "Biomet's Contrarian Conservatism," 53.
10. Ibid.
11. Ibid.
12. Ibid., 54.
13. Ibid.
14. Ibid.
15. Kolter, interview.
16. Ibid.
17. Eric Martin, interviewed by Jeffrey L. Rodengen, tape recording, 18 May 2001, Write Stuff Enterprises.
18. Kolter, interview.
19. Ibid.
20. Ibid.
21. Ibid.
22. *Bio Briefs*, fall/winter 1995, 1.
23. Jessica Hall, "Torn between two bidders: Kirschner's enviable dilemma," *Warfield's Business Record*, 1 July 1994, Vol. 9, No. 26, Sec. 1, 3.
24. Jessica Hall, "Third suitor jumps in bidding war for Kirschner Medical," *Warfield's Business Record*, 15 July 1994, Vol. 9, No. 28, Sec. 1, 3.

25. Jessica Hall, "Kirschner accepts deal with orthopedics giant to end seven-week bidding war," *Warfield's Business Record,* 22 July 1994, Vol. 9, No. 29, Sec. 1, 11.
26. Jay Margolis, "Biomet signs merger deal with Kirschner," *Fort Wayne Journal Gazette,* 19 July 1994, Sec. C, 1.
27. *Bio Briefs,* fall/winter 1995, 1.
28. Biomet 1995 Annual Report, 10.
29. Biomet 1997 Annual Report, 18.
30. *Bio Briefs,* fall/winter 1995, 1.
31. Ibid., 5.
32. Ibid., 1.
33. *Bio Briefs,* summer 1994, 1.
34. Biomet 1994 Annual Report, 2.
35. Ibid., 14.
36. Ibid.
37. *Bio Briefs,* winter 1994, 1.
38. Biomet 1994 Annual Report, 14.
39. Ibid.
40. Ibid., 24.
41. Biomet 1995 Annual Report, 2.
42. Ibid., 13.
43. Ibid., 2.
44. Ibid.
45. Ibid.
46. Ibid., 13.
47. *Bio Briefs,* fall 1995, 1.
48. Jerry Ferguson, interview.
49. *Bio Briefs,* fall 1995, 1.

Chapter Six Sidebar: Hungry for Knowledge

1. Lance Perry, interviewed by Richard F. Hubbard, tape recording, 30 August 2001, Write Stuff Enterprises.
2. "Biomet's Web Site Wins Award," *Times-Union,* 28 September 1996.
3. Perry, interview.
4. Paula Hoesel, interviewed by Richard F. Hubbard, tape recording, 20 November 2001, Write Stuff Enterprises.

Chapter Seven

1. "Biomet to pay dividend," *South Bend Tribune,* 28 September 1996.
2. Biomet 1996 Annual Report, 3.
3. Ibid., 1.
4. Ibid., 3.
5. Ibid.
6. *Bio Briefs,* winter 1996, 1.
7. Biomet 1996 Annual Report, 1.
8. Biomet 1997 Annual Report, 20.
9. Biomet 1996 Annual Report, 31.
10. "Surgeon Wins Patent Suit," *Phoenix Gazette,* 26 January 1996, E1.
11. "Verdicts Reduced After Trial," *The National Law Journal,* 10 February 1997, C11.
12. Ibid.

13. "Surgeon Awarded $55.45M For Patent Infringement," *The National Law Journal,* 19 February 1996, A11.
14. Ibid.
15. "Analysts Say Judgment Shouldn't Hurt Biomet," *South Bend Tribune,* 27 January 1996.
16. Hann, interview.
17. Biomet 1999 Annual Report, 46.
18. Biomet 2001 Annual Report, 45.
19. Business Wire, Press Release, 10 November 1988.
20. Brad Tandy, interviewed by Richard F. Hubbard, tape recording, 29 August 2001, Write Stuff Enterprises.
21. *Bio Briefs,* summer 1996, 1.
22. Ibid.
23. Biomet 1998 Annual Report, 42.
24. Biomet 2001 Annual Report, 45.
25. Biomet 1997 Annual Report, 2.
26. Ibid.
27. Ibid., 22, 10–11.
28. Ibid., 12.
29. Kurowski, "Industrialist of the Year," 48.

Chapter Seven Sidebar: Biomet on Wheels

1. Norm Hagg, "Biomet Racing: Local orthopedic company expands into Busch

circuit," *Times-Union*, 17 May 1977; "Biomet Sponsors Indy Car," *Times-Union*, 18 May 1995.
2. Mary Louise Miller, interview.

Chapter Eight

1. Michael J. Pachuta, "Biomet Sees an Opportunity in a Consolidating Industry," *Investor's Business Daily*, 24 June 1999, 18.
2. Ibid.
3. Ibid.
4. Biomet 1998 Annual Report, 34.
5. "Biomet and Merck KGaA Announce Intent to Form Joint Venture," Business Wire, 19 May 1997.
6. Press Release, 2 February 1998, Merck KGaA.
7. *Bio Briefs*, March 1998, 2.
8. Press Release, 2 February 1998, Merck KGaA.
9. Securities and Exchange Commission Form, 31 May 2000, 32.
10. Biomet 1999 Annual Report, 13.
11. Wagoner, interview.
12. Ibid.
13. Ibid.
14. Biomet 1999 Annual Report, 13.
15. Press Release, 24 November 1998, Merck KGaA.

16. Biomet 1998 Annual Report, 4–5.
17. Ibid., 13.
18. Biomet 1999 Annual Report, 5.
19. Biomet 1998 Annual Report, 2.
20. Ibid.
21. Ibid.
22. Ibid.
23. Ibid.
24. Ibid., 3.
25. Ibid., 10.
26. "Comprehensive Orthopedics Industry Report Published by U.S. Bancorp Piper Jaffray," Business Wire, 29 July 1999.
27. *Bio Briefs*, summer 1999, 1.
28. Craig Blaschke, interviewed by Jeffrey L. Rodengen, tape recording, 18 May 2001, Write Stuff Enterprises.
29. Ibid.
30. Joel Higgins, interviewed by Richard F. Hubbard, 30 August 2001, tape recording, Write Stuff Enterprises.
31. Information provided by Craig Blaschke to Heather Deeley, May 2002.
32. Biomet 2000 Annual Report, 5.
33. Ibid., 38.
34. Ibid., 21.
35. Ibid.
36. Keith Beaty, interviewed by Richard F. Hubbard,

tape recording, 12 November 2001, Write Stuff Enterprises.
37. Biomet 1999 Annual Report, 3.
38. Biomet 2001 Annual Report, 20.
39. Ibid.
40. Biomet 2000 Annual Report, 21.
41. Ibid.
42. Ibid.
43. Ibid.
44. Ibid.

Chapter Eight Sidebar: A Brief History of Merck

1. http://www.merck.de/english/corporate/index.htm, 2001.

Chapter Nine

1. Biomet 2000 Annual Report, 3.
2. Lonnie Witham, interviewed by Richard F. Hubbard, tape recording, 2 November 2001, Write Stuff Enterprises.
3. Biomet 2000 Annual Report, 3.
4. Ibid., 13.
5. Ibid.
6. Ibid.
7. John Repicci, D.D.S, M.D., interviewed by Richard F. Hubbard, tape recording, 9 November 2001, Write Stuff Enterprises.
8. Perry, interview.
9. Biomet 2000 Annual Report, 3.

10. Ibid.
11. Biomet Press Release, 25 September 2000; *Bio Briefs*, fall 2000, 1.
12. Ibid.
13. Ibid.
14. Ibid.
15. Sasso, interview.
16. Biomet Press Release, 25 September 2000.
17. Biomet 2000 Annual Report, 13.
18. Business Wire, 22 May 2000.
19. Ibid.
20. "M²a-Taper Metal-on-Metal Articulation," Biomet sales brochure, 2000.
21. Ibid.
22. Ibid.
23. Ibid.
24. Ibid.
25. Ibid.
26. Biomet 2000 Annual Report, 42.
27. Business Wire, 6 July 2000.
28. Biomet 2001 Annual Report, 5.
29. "Musculoskeletal medical," WSCR.com, 25 September–1 October, 2000, 25.
30. Biomet 2001 Annual Report, 2.
31. Ibid., 3.
32. Biomet Press Release, www.biomet.com, 6 December 2001.
33. "Z-KAT Announces Strategic Alliance with Biomet, Inc.," Press Release, 5 February 2002.
34. Ibid.
35. Biomet 2001 Annual Report,www.biomet.com.
36. Ibid.
37. Dane Miller, interview.
38. Robert Ronk, interviewed by Richard F. Hubbard, tape recording, 29 August 2001,Write Stuff Enterprises.
39. John Cuckler, M.D., interviewed by Richard F. Hubbard, tape recording, 30 November 2001, Write Stuff Enterprises.
40. Ibid.
41. England, interview.
42. Hershberger, interview.
43. Higgins, interview.
44. Pratt, interview.
45. John Susaraba, interviewed by Richard F. Hubbard, tape recording, 17 May 2001, Write Stuff Enterprises.
46. Cuckler, interview.
47. Steve Watkins, "Metal Hip Joints Could Put Spring in Sales," *Investor's Business Daily,* 2000.
48. Dan Williamson, interviewed by Richard F. Hubbard, tape recording, 17 May 2001, Write Stuff Enterprises.

**Chapter Nine Sidebar:
The Oxford Meniscal Knee**

1. Um M. Young, "Knee patient walks the next day; unicompartmental arthroplasty may be the way of the future," *Canadian Business and Current Affairs,* 23 January 2001, 5.

**Chapter Nine Sidebar:
Bone-Deep Value**

1. James E. Ellis, "You don't necessarily get what you pay for," *Business Week,* 4 May 1992.
2. Ibid.
3. Jerry Ferguson, interview.
4. Hoover's Online.
5. Jerry Ferguson, interview.

**Chapter Nine Sidebar:
Recession Resistant**

1. Debra Sherman, "Indiana city thrives on artificial joints," Reuters U.S. Company News, 9 December 2001.

**Chapter Nine Sidebar:
Best Thing since Sliced Bread**

1. Ted Dobbins, interviewed by Richard F. Hubbard, tape recording, 19 November 2001, Write Stuff Enterprises.
2. Ibid.
3. Ibid.

INDEX